STEAMPUNK
COLORING BO

MW01269217

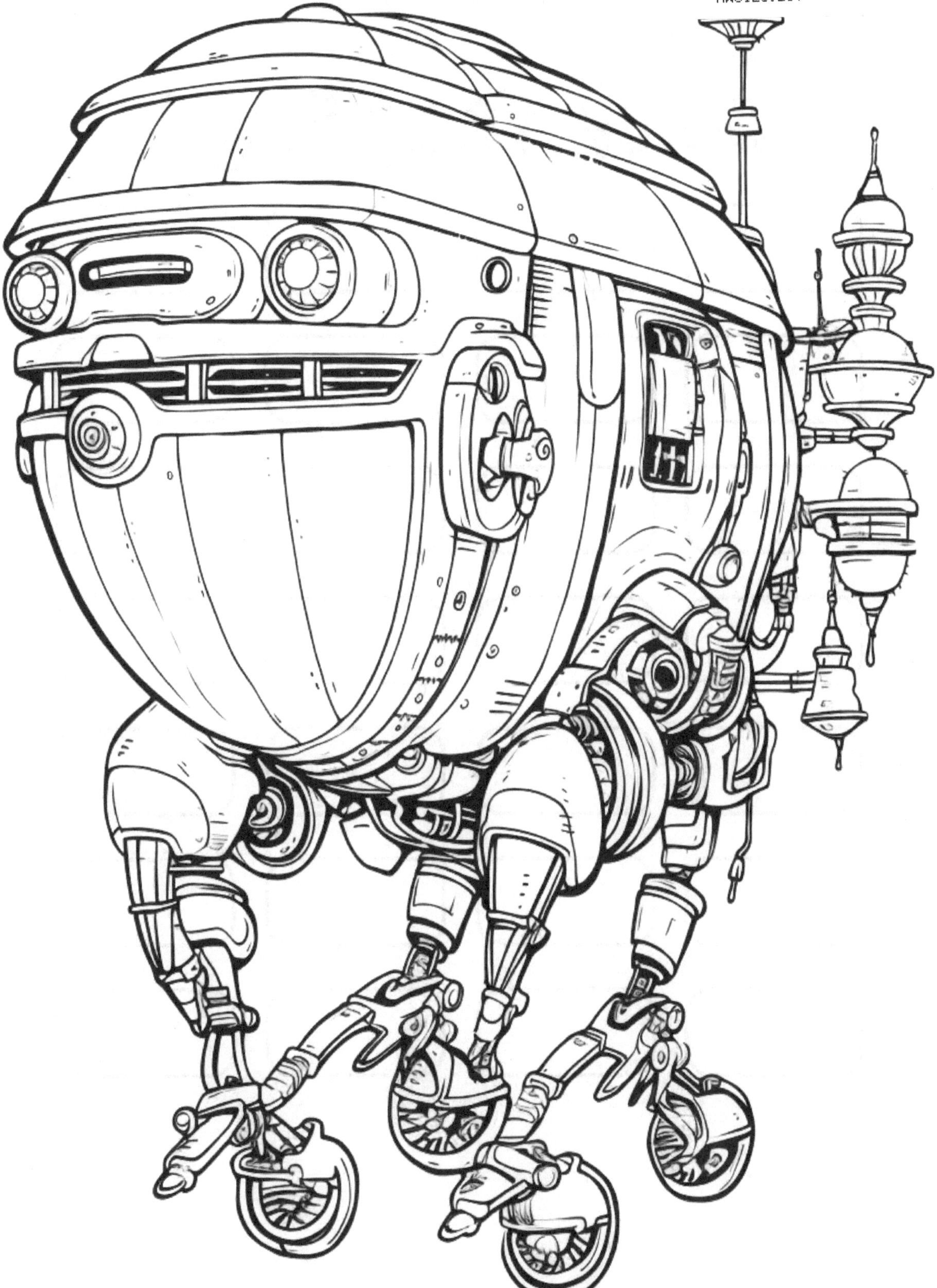

This Book Belongs To

Color Test Page

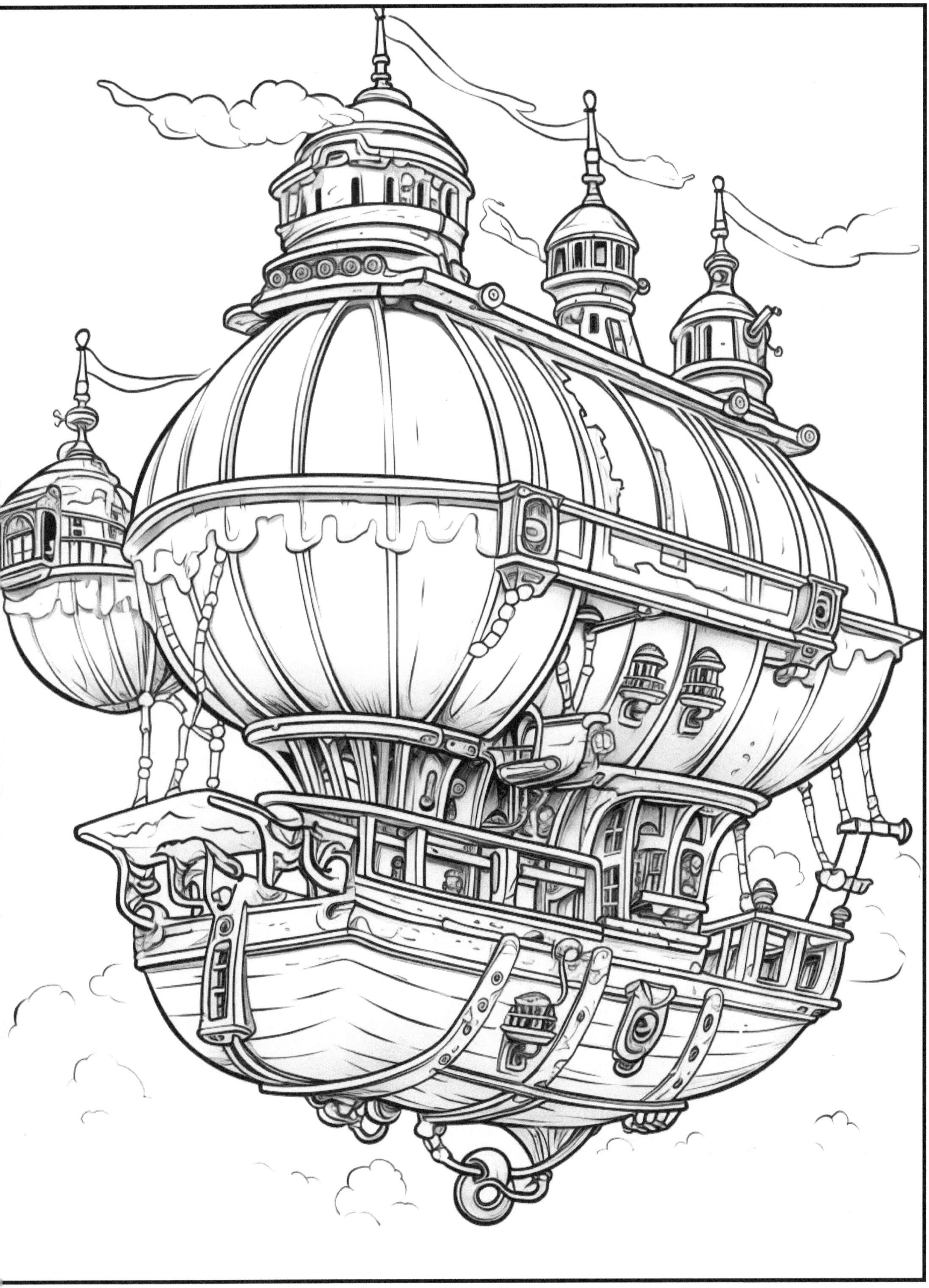

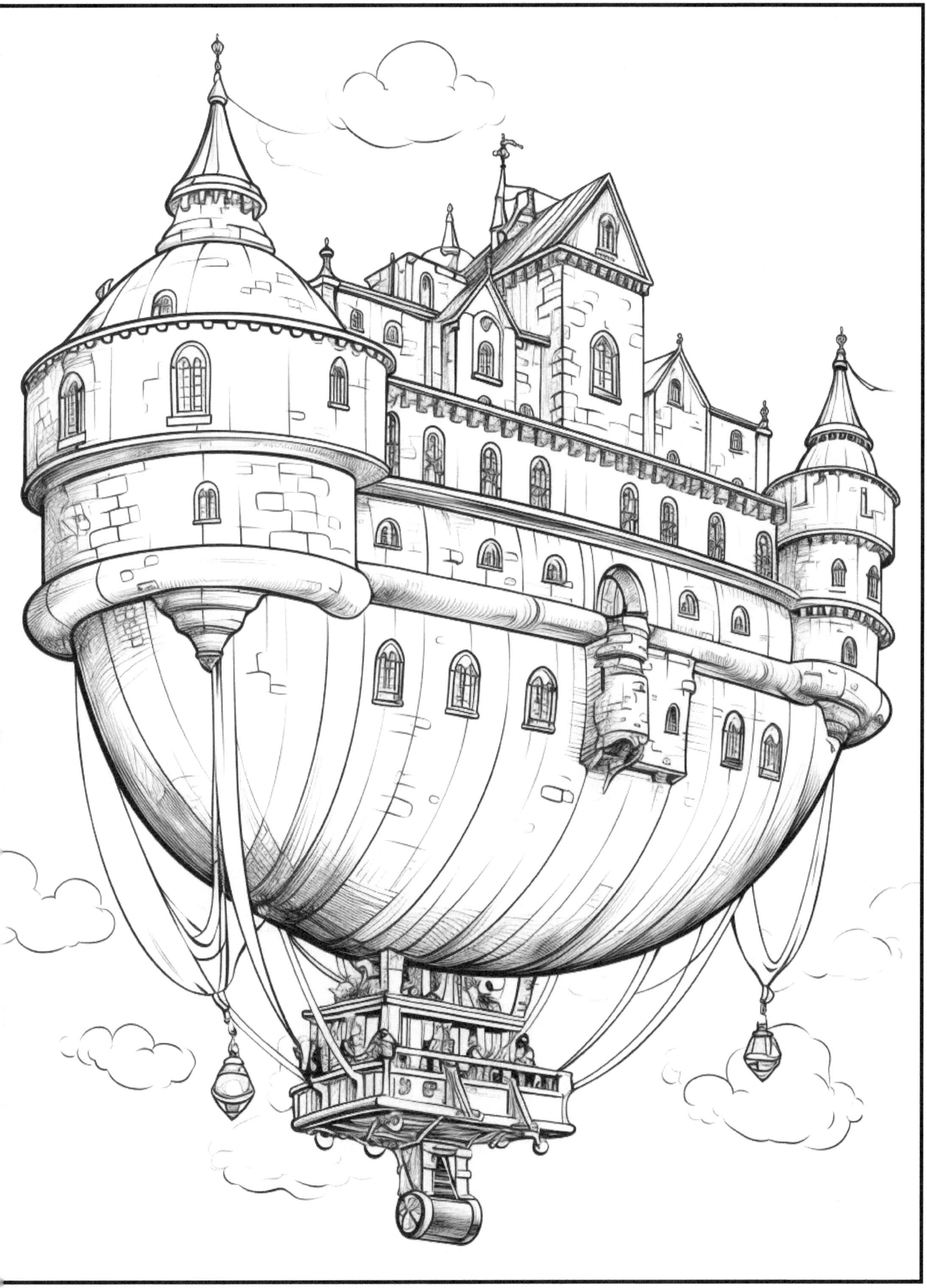

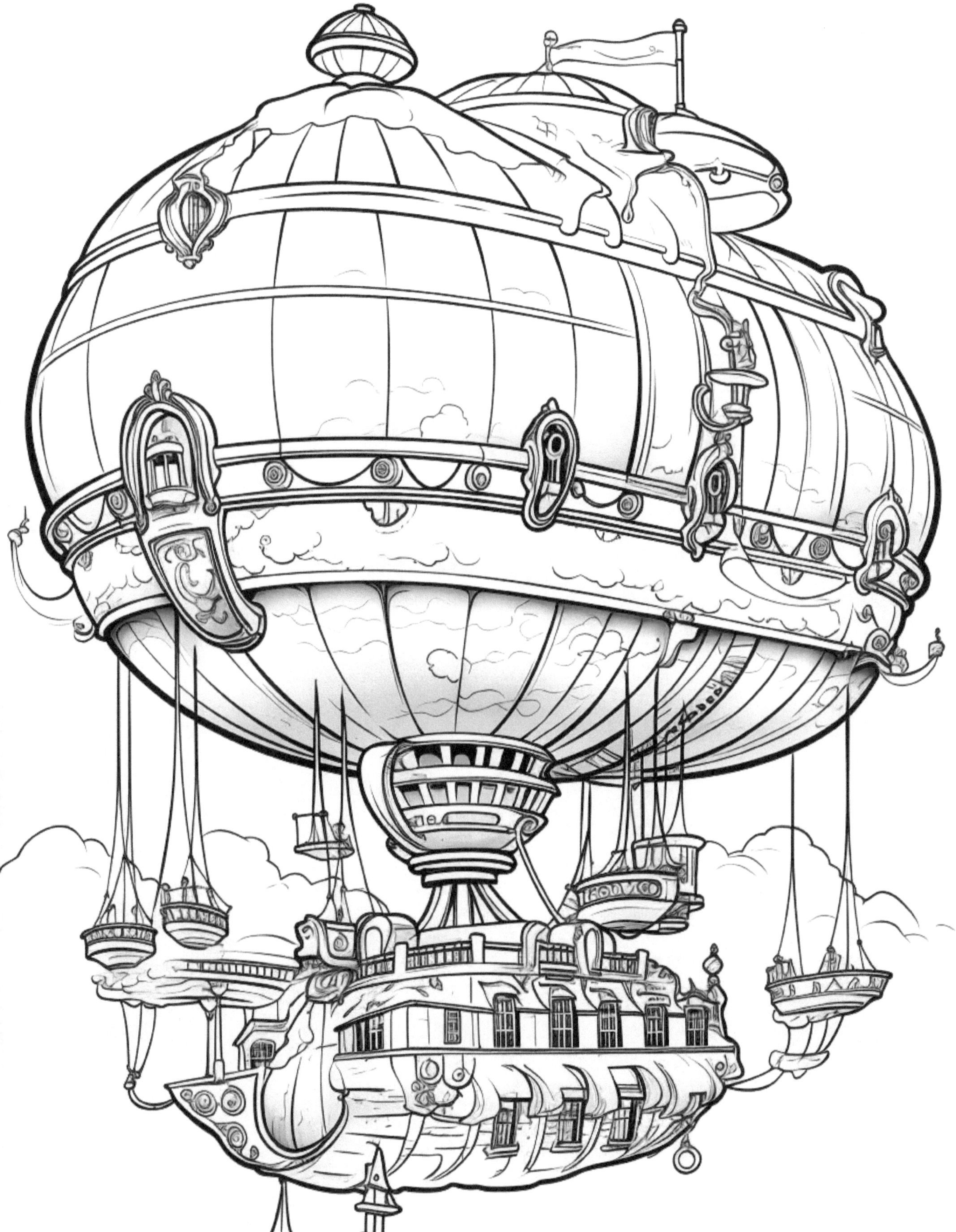

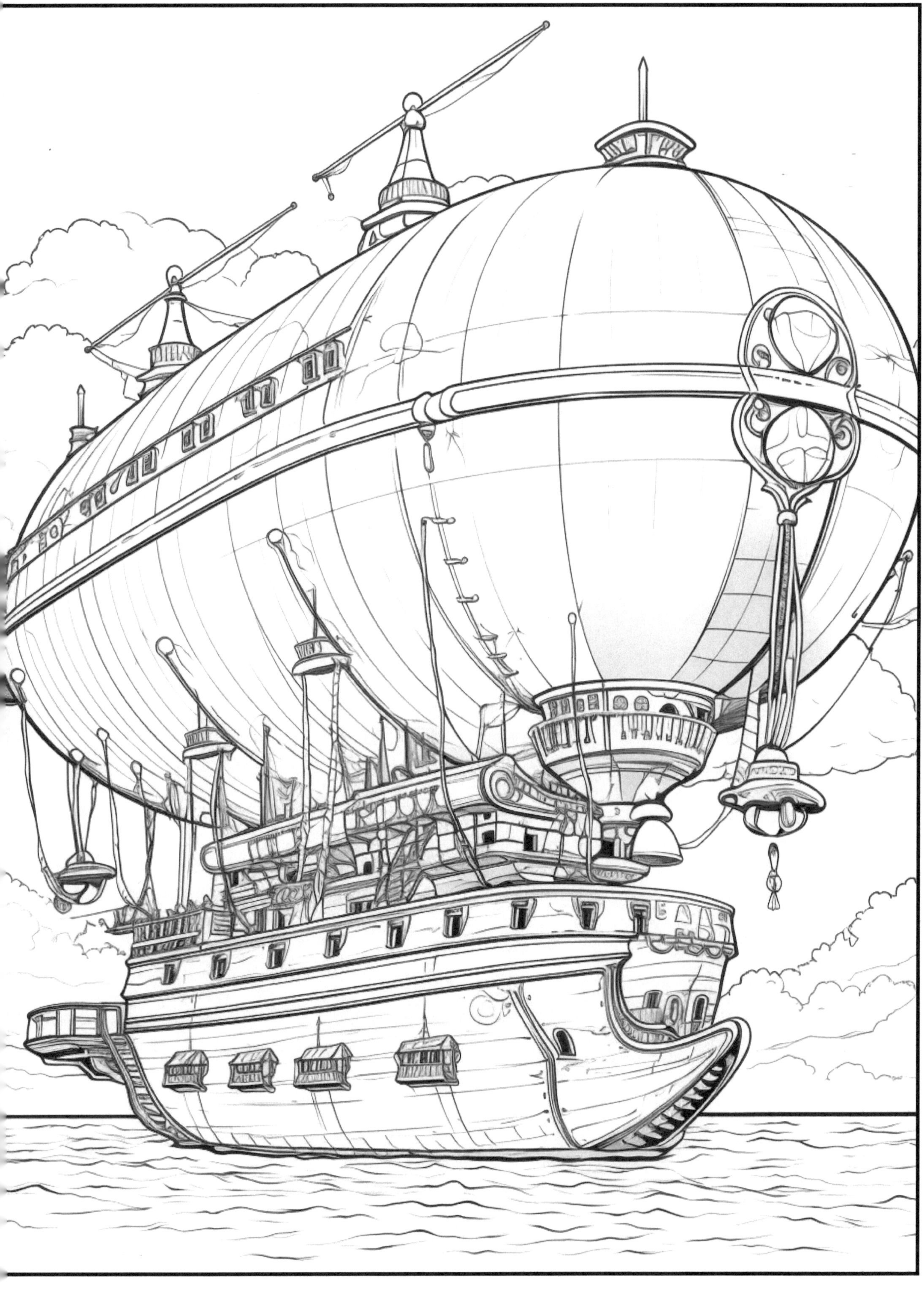

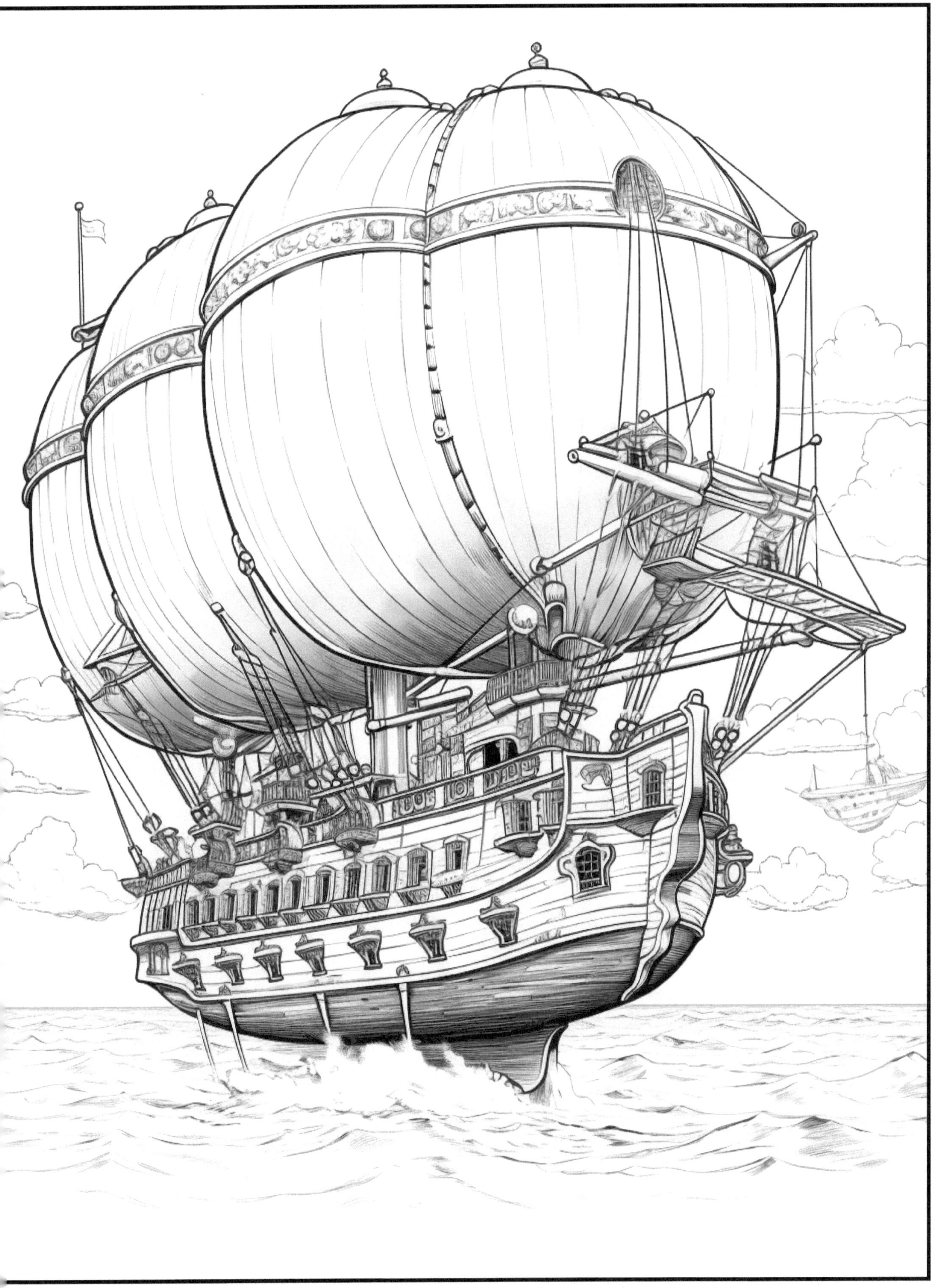

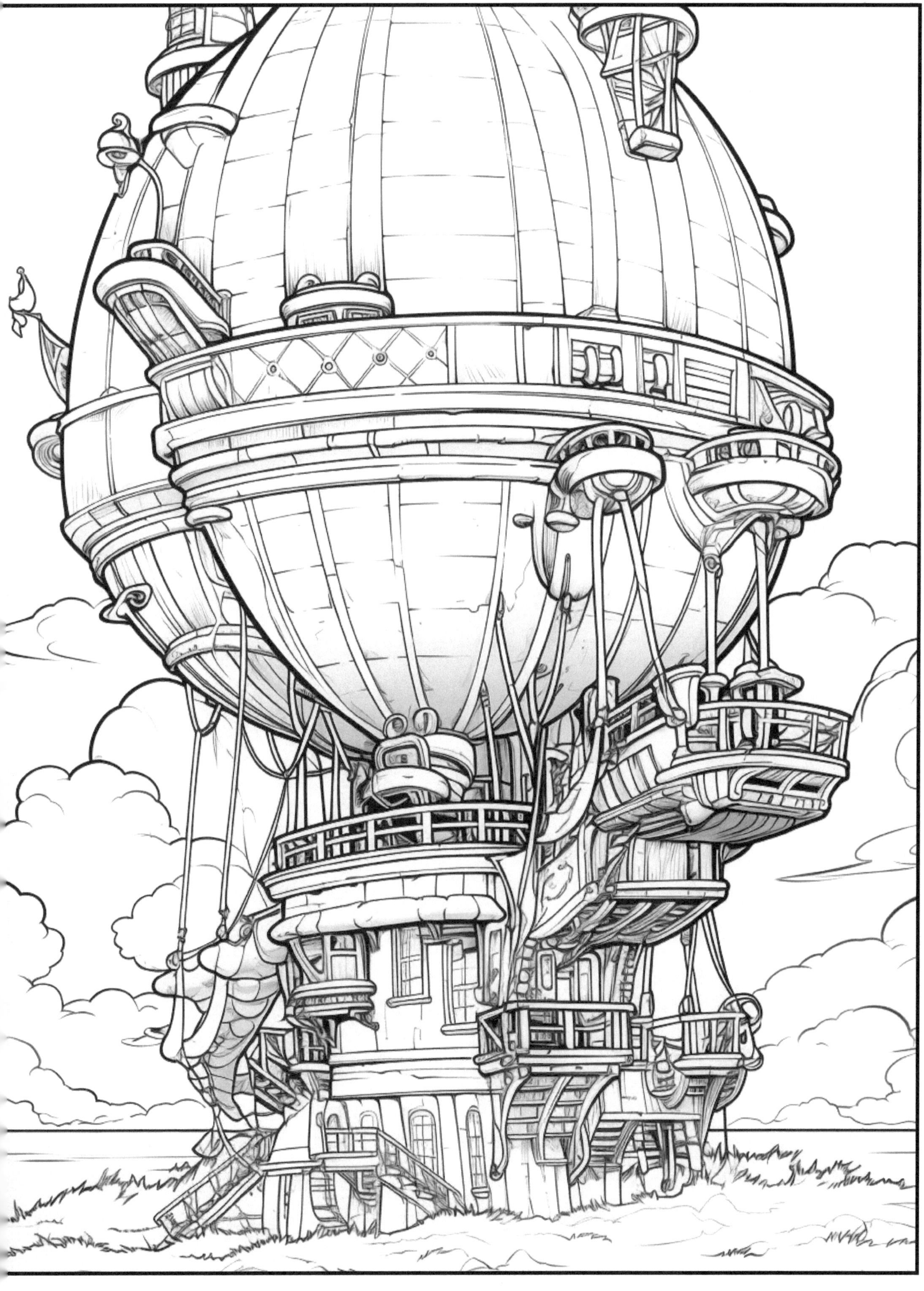

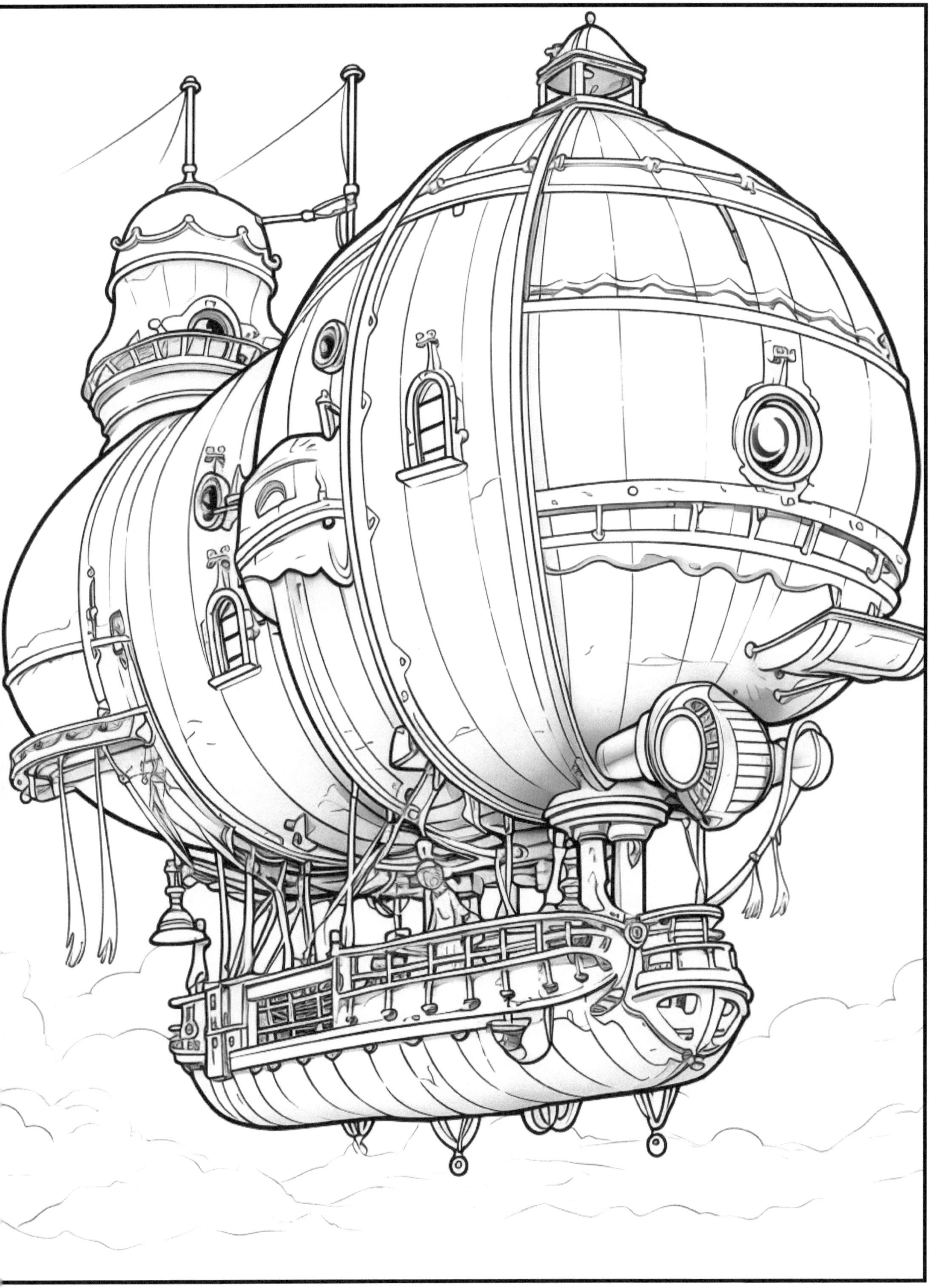

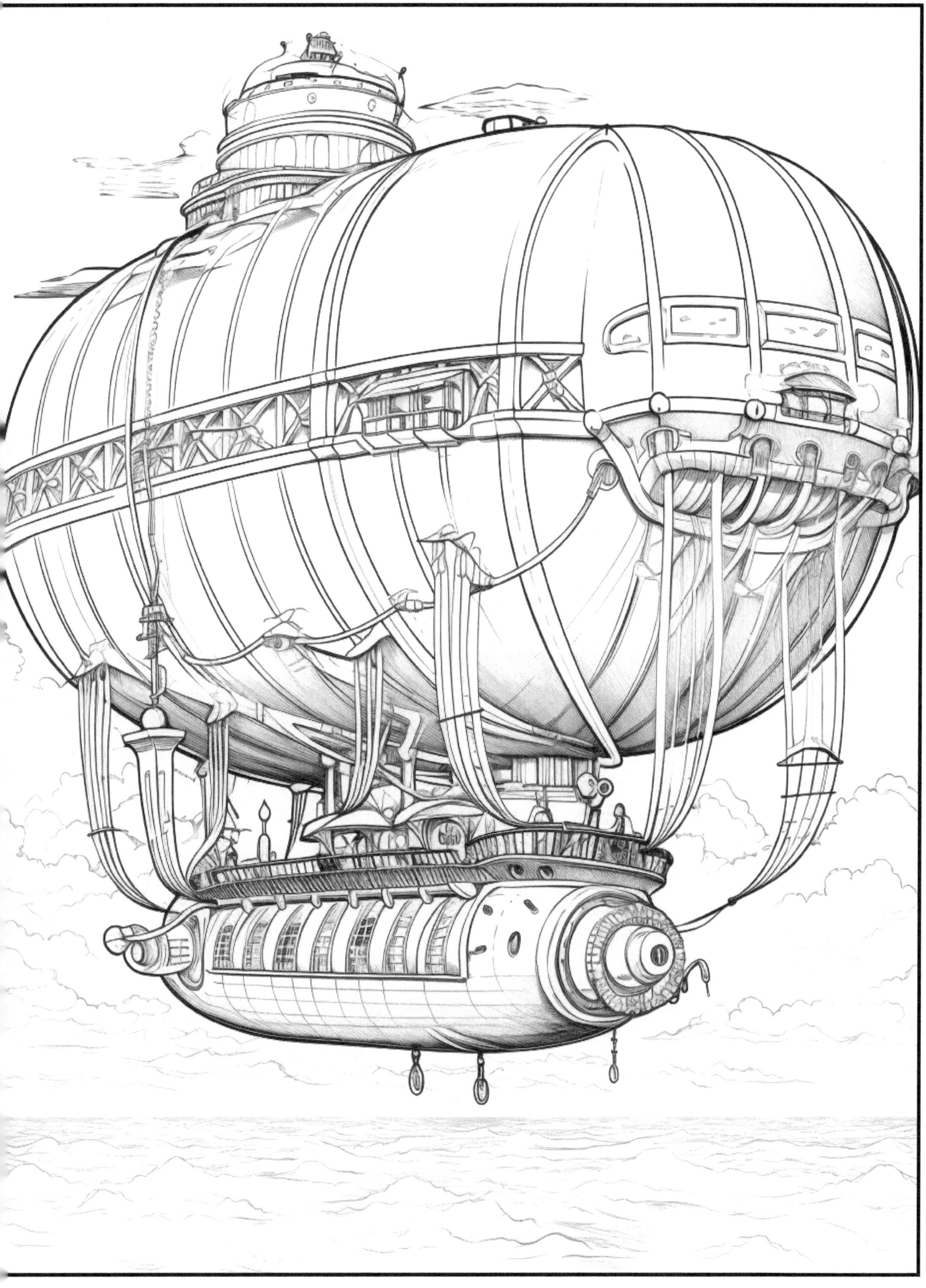

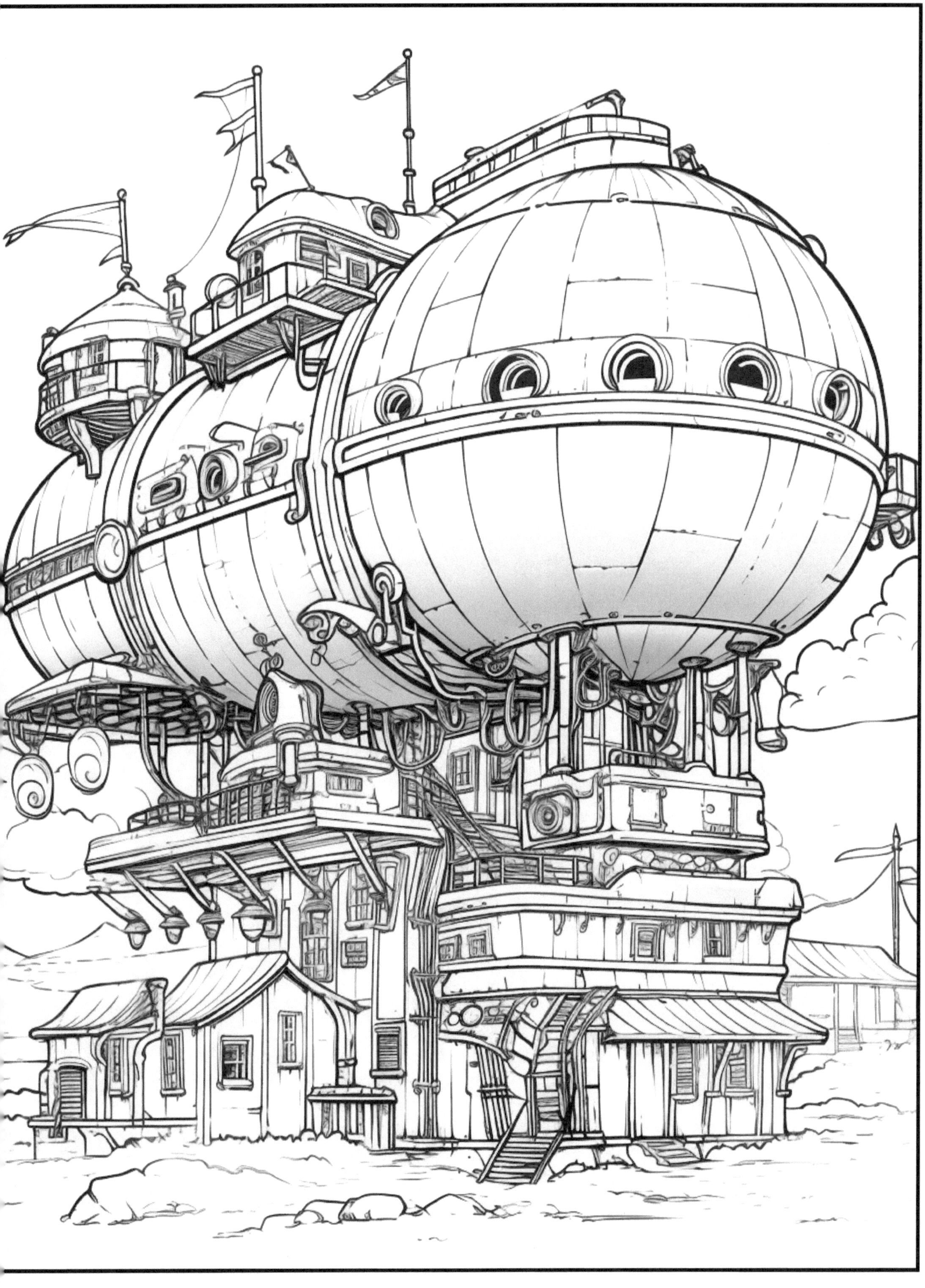

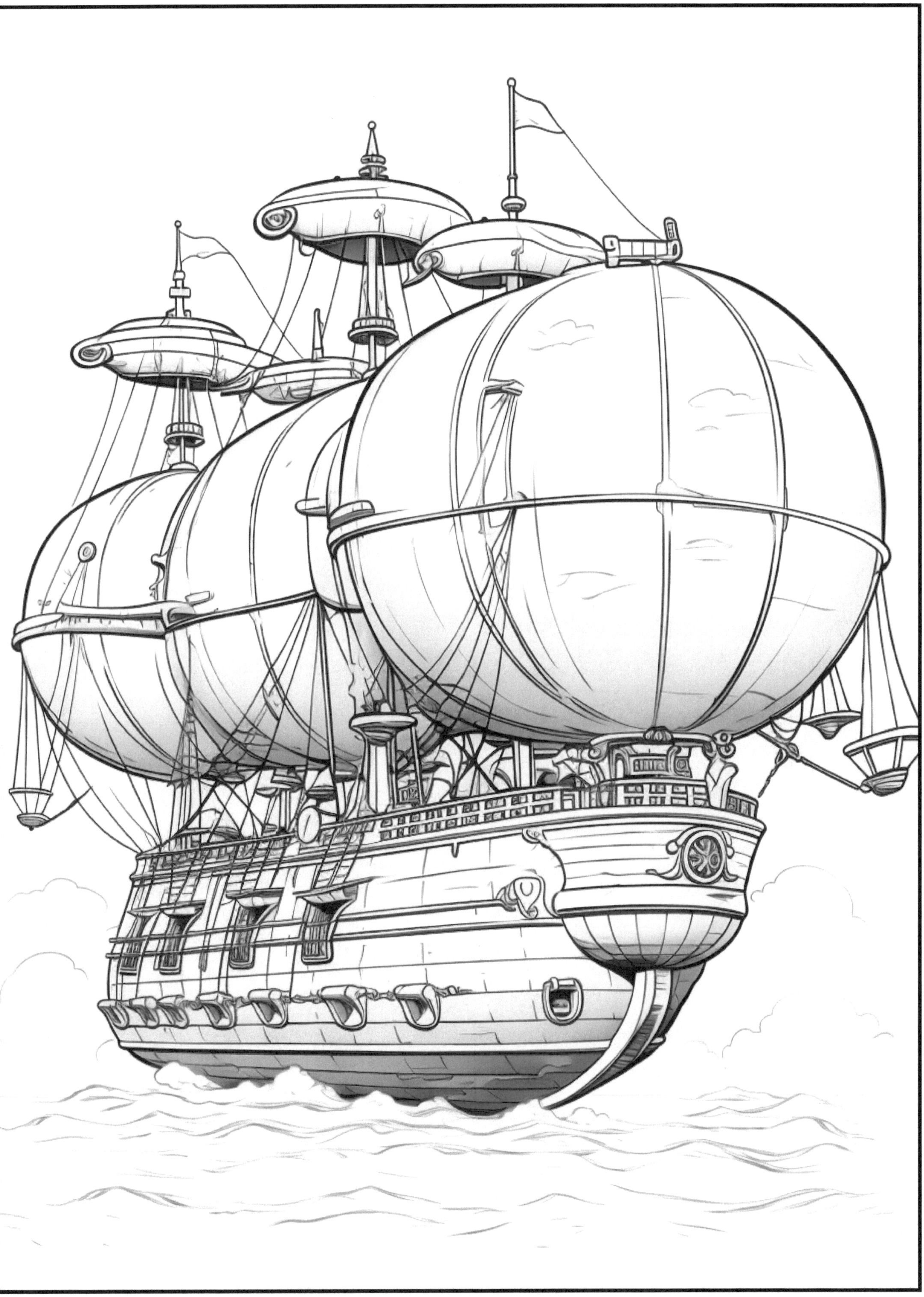

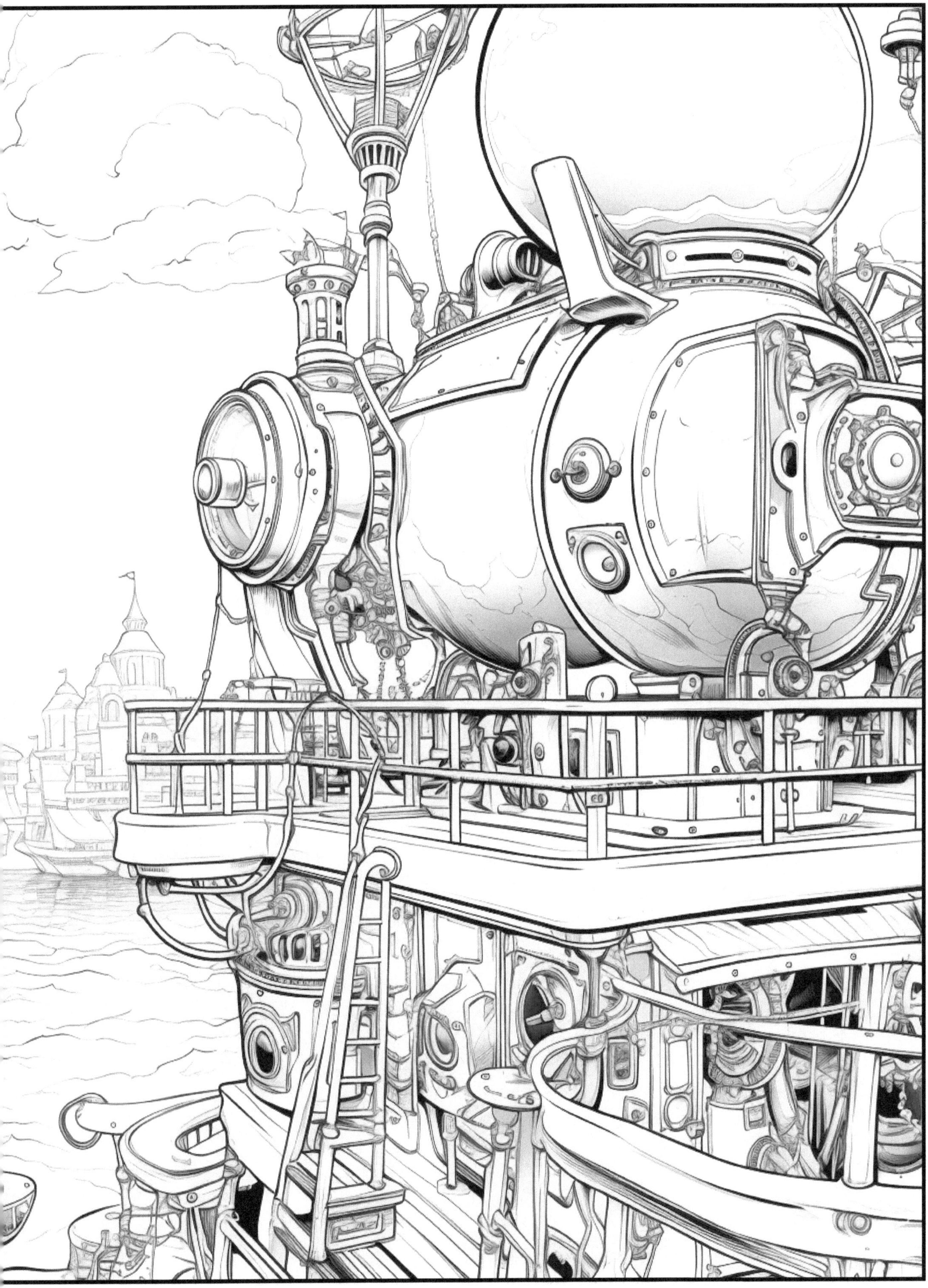

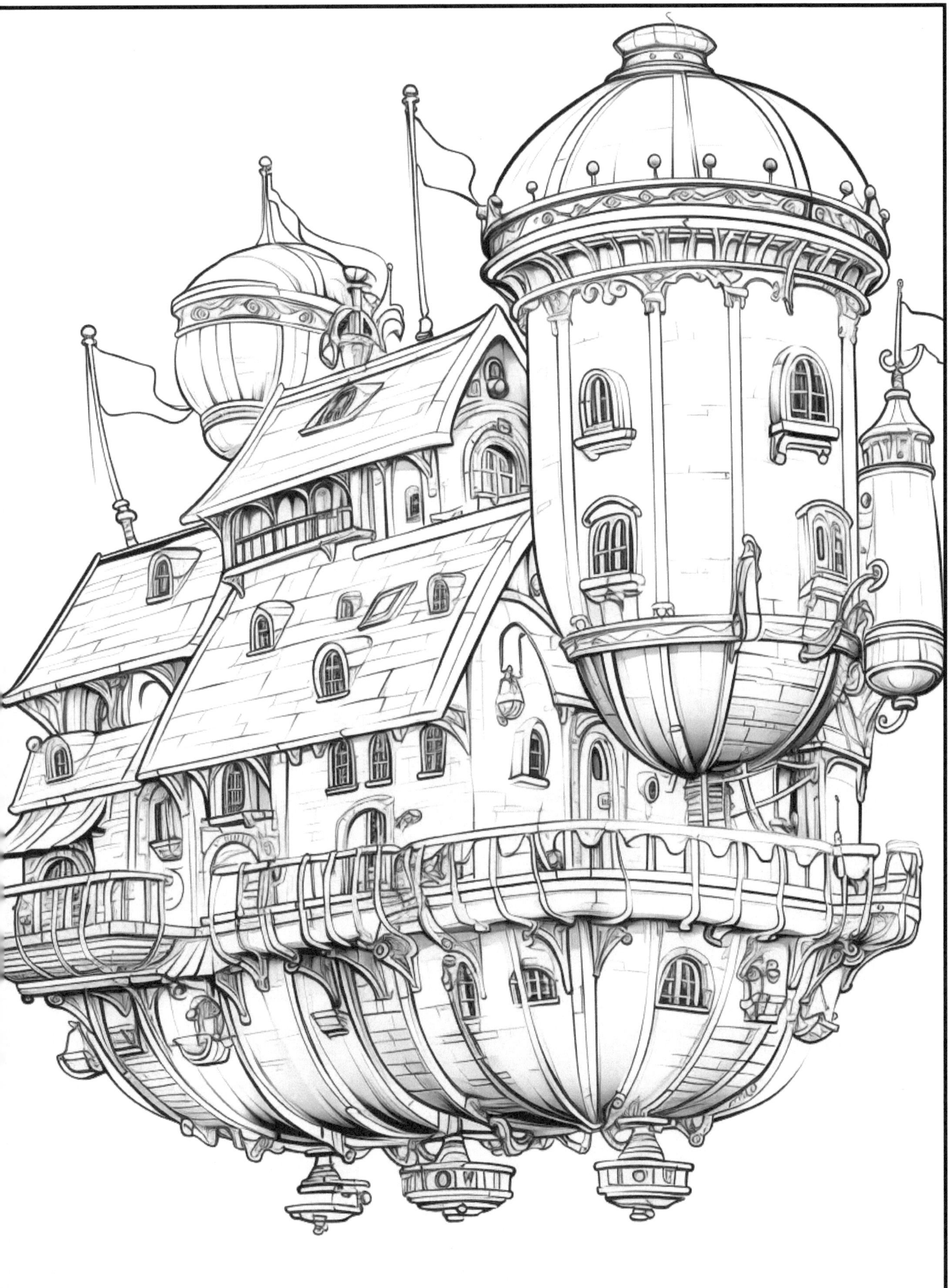

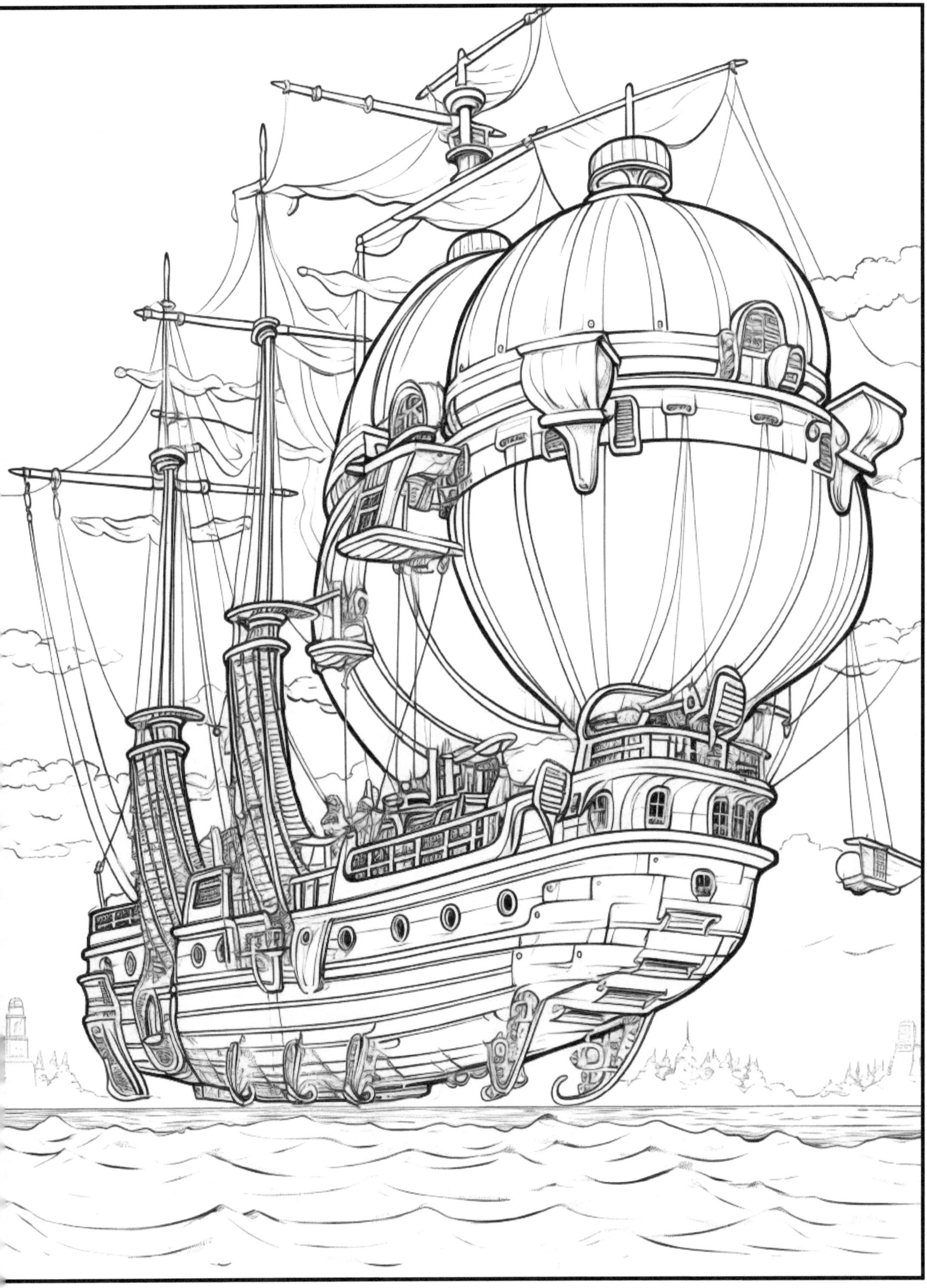

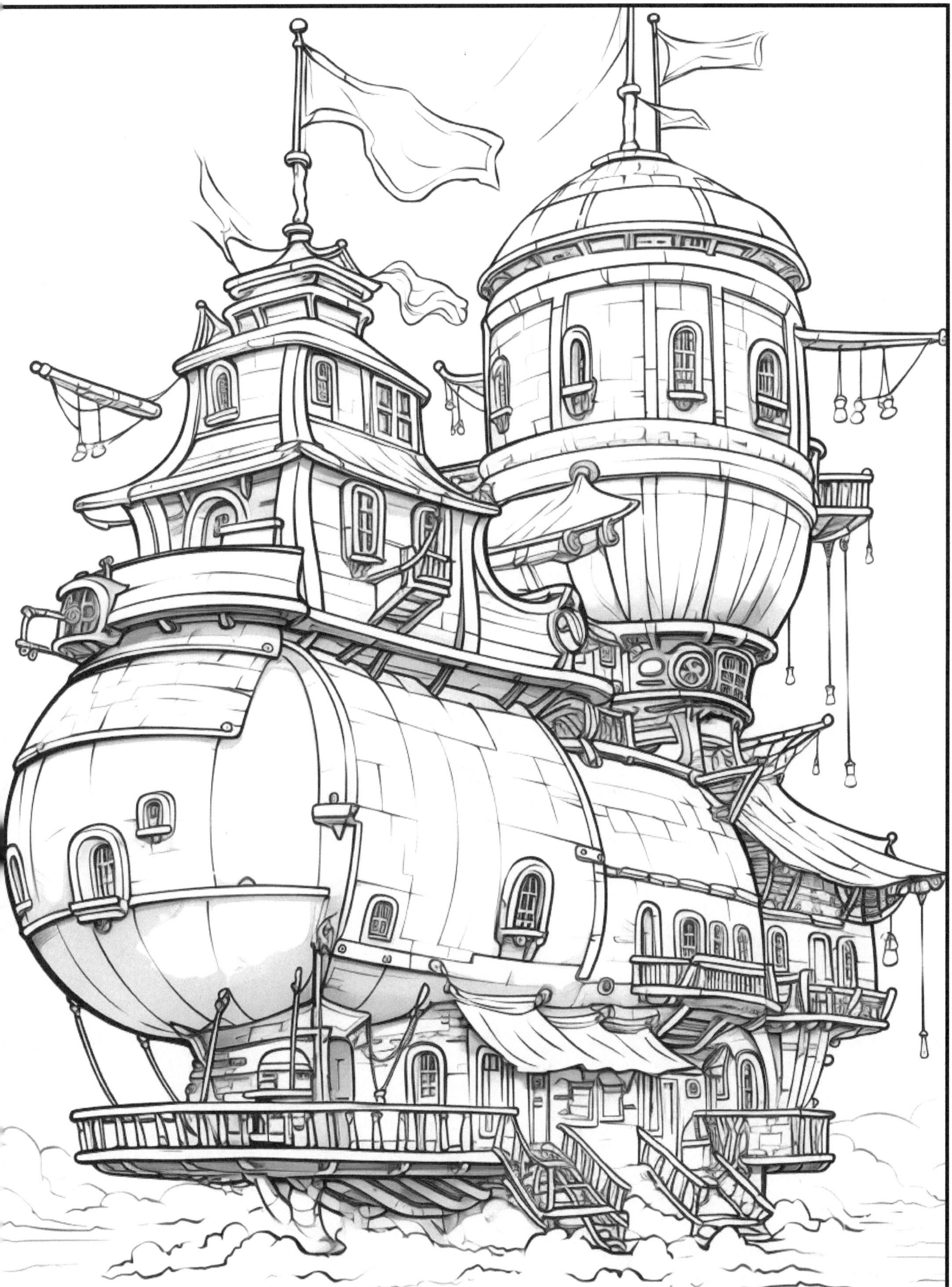

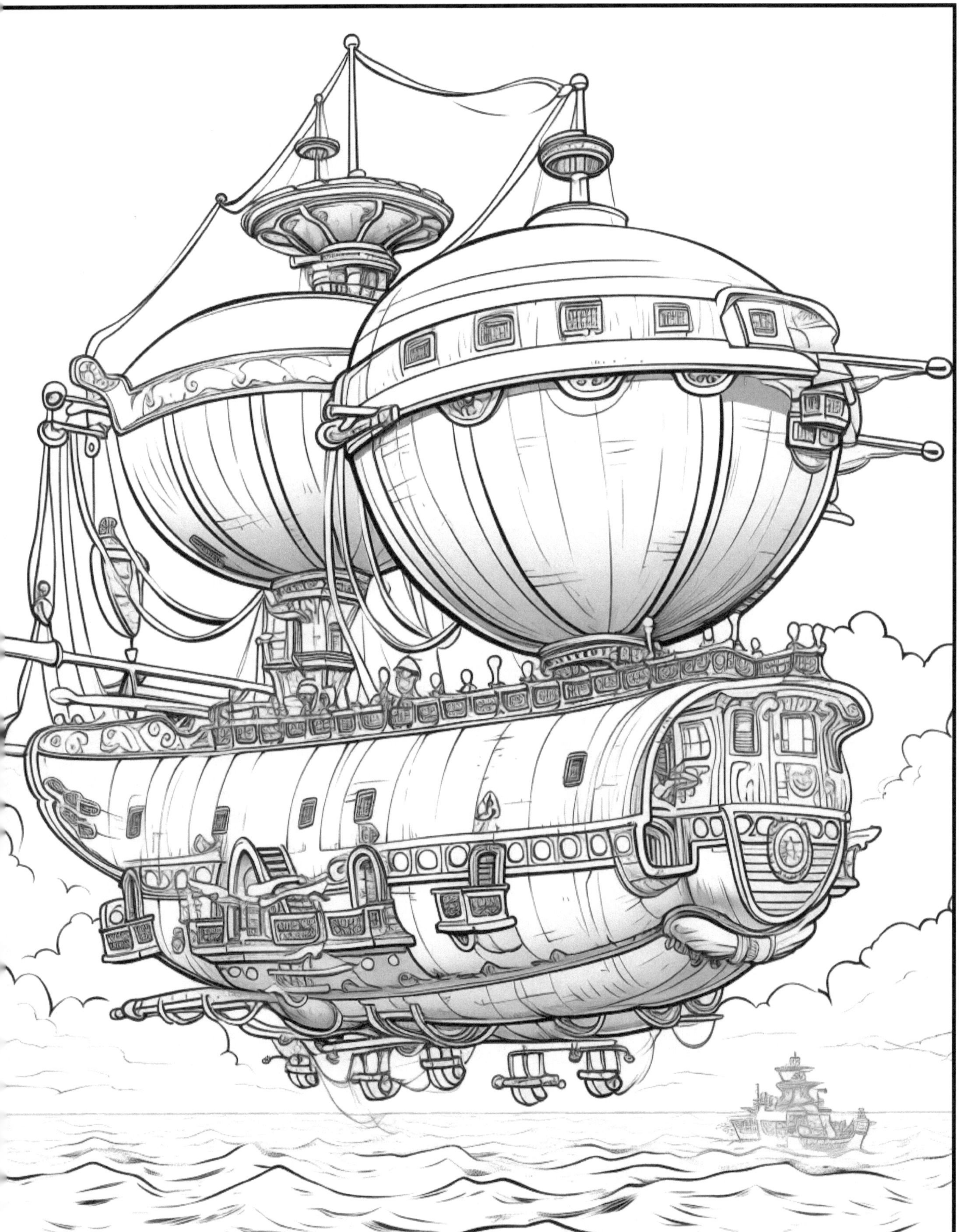

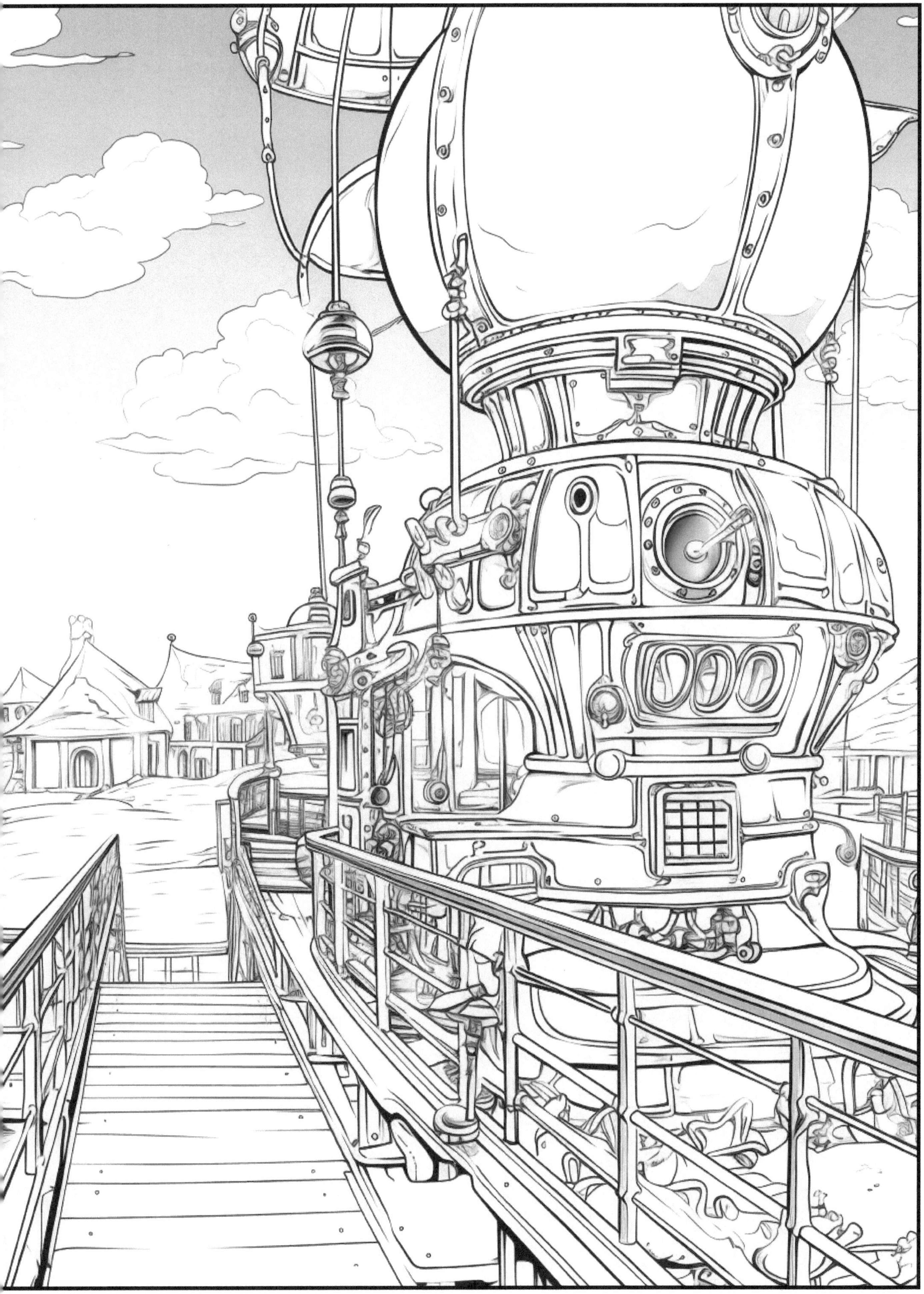

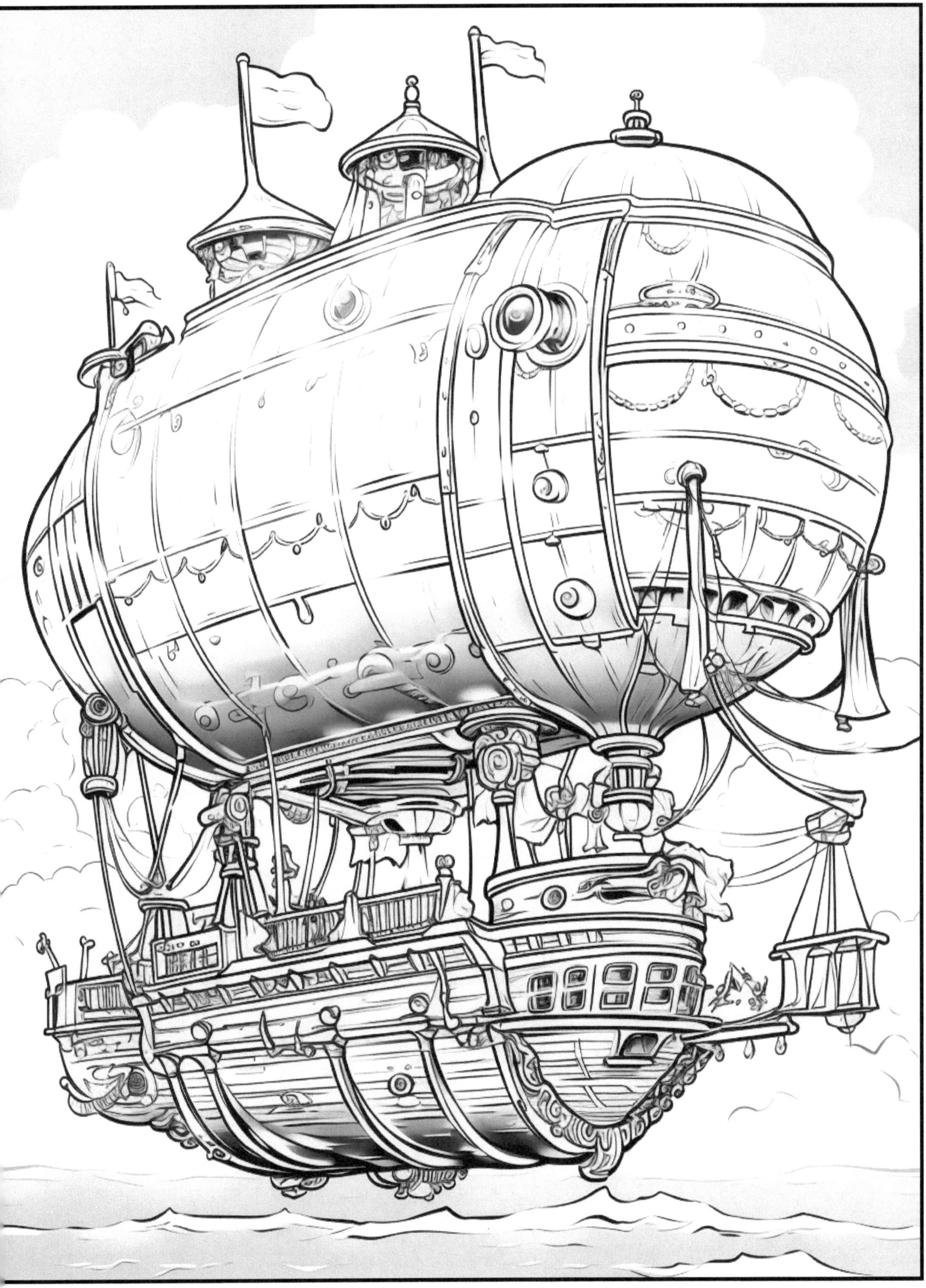

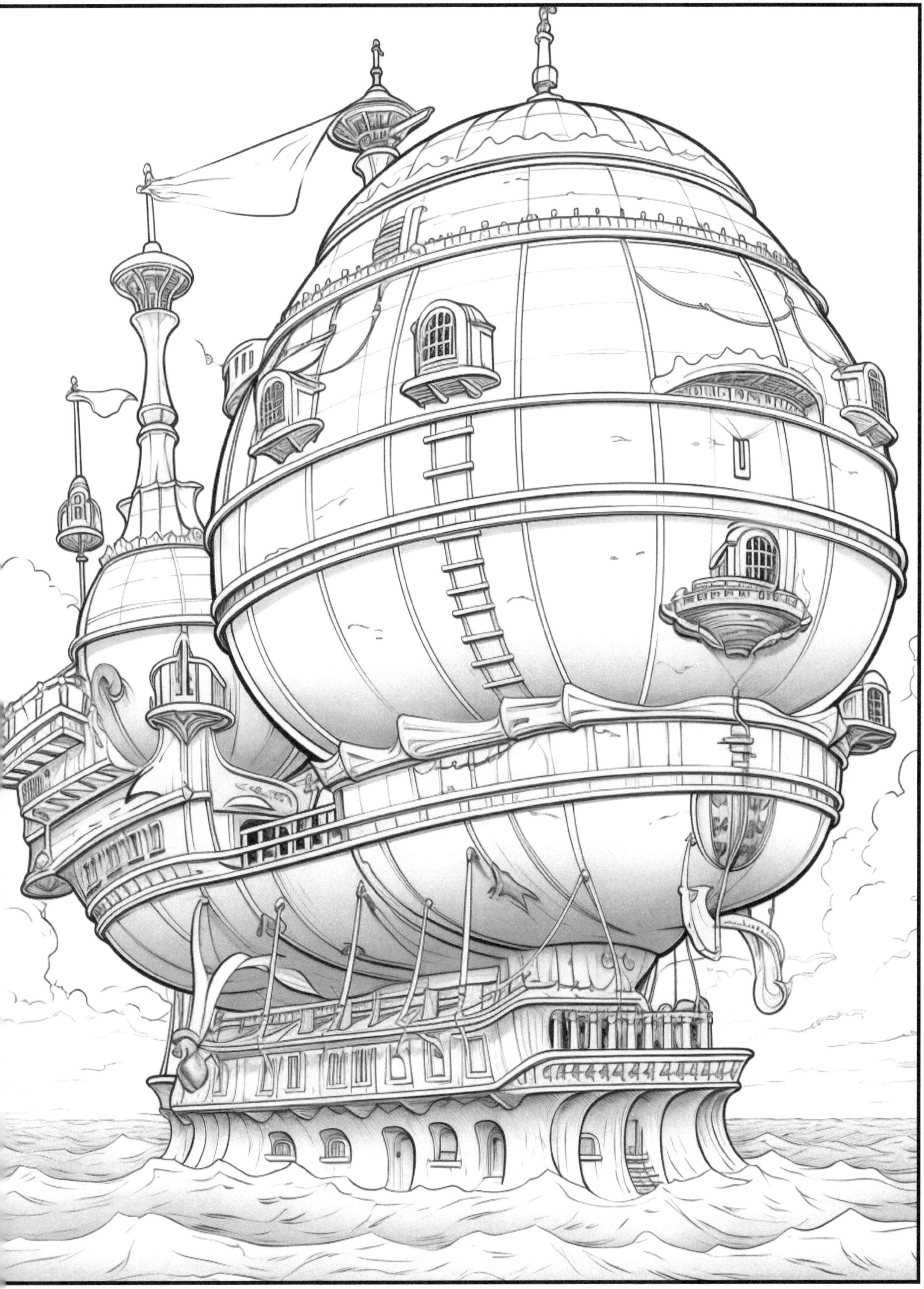

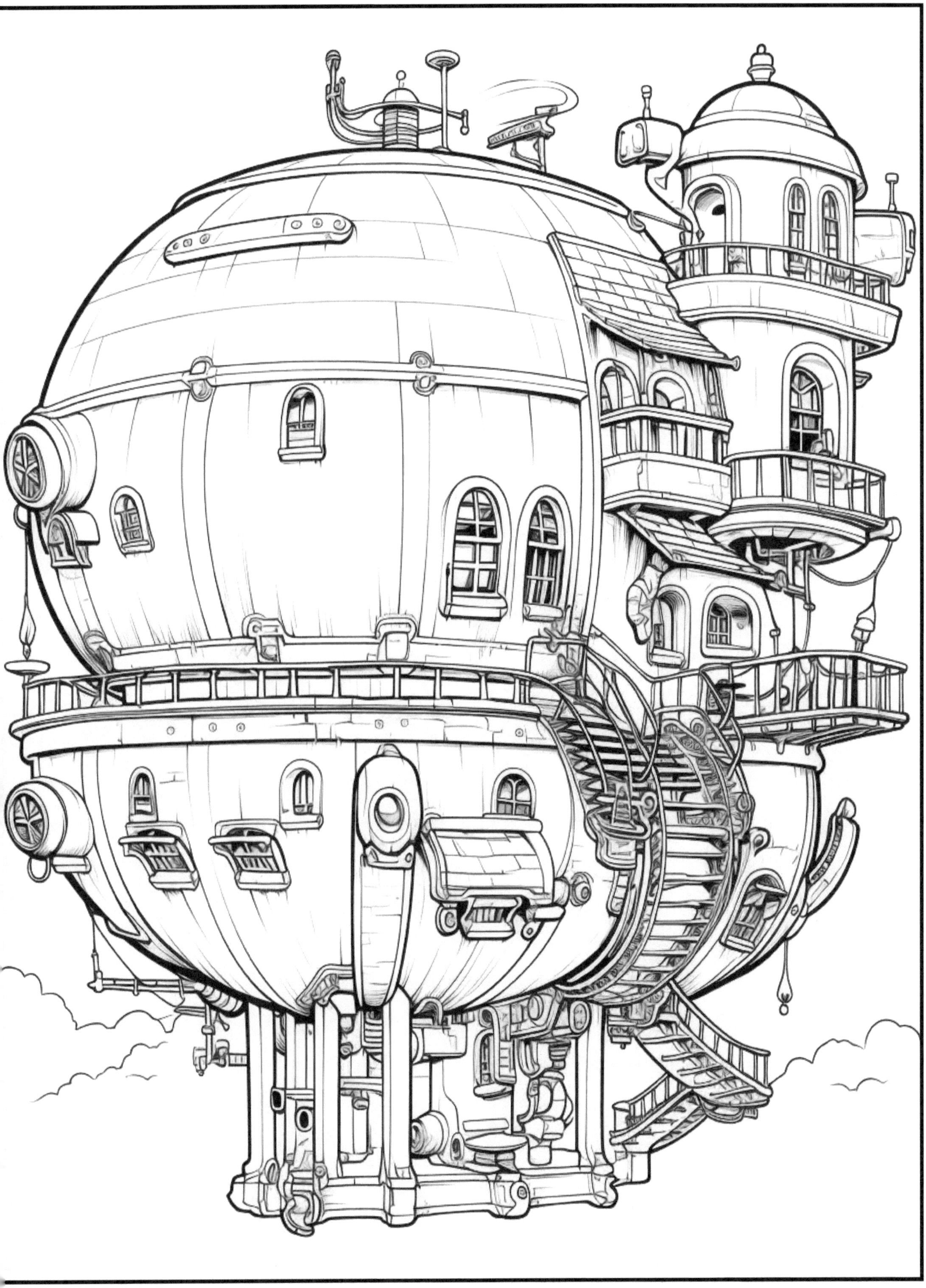

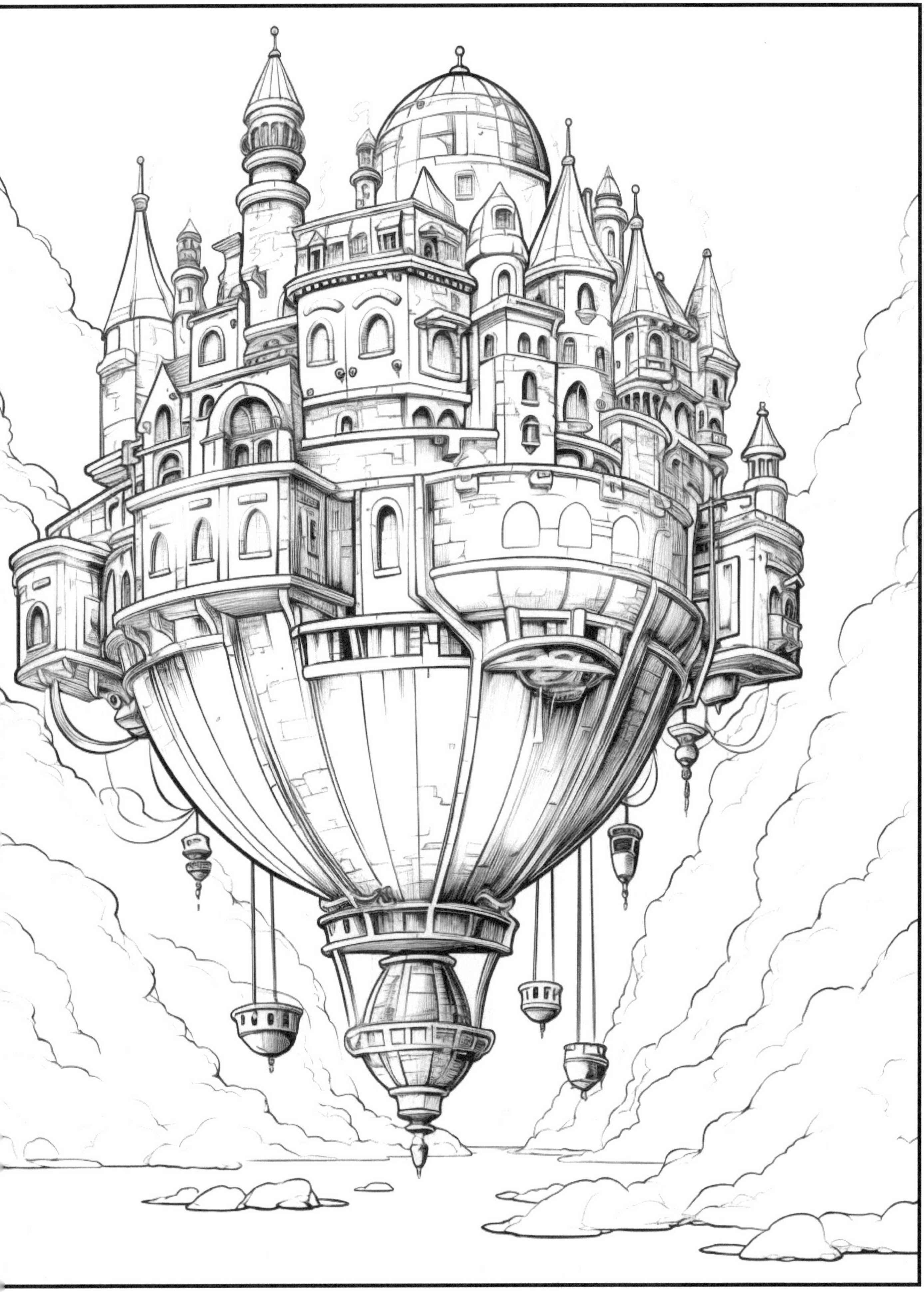

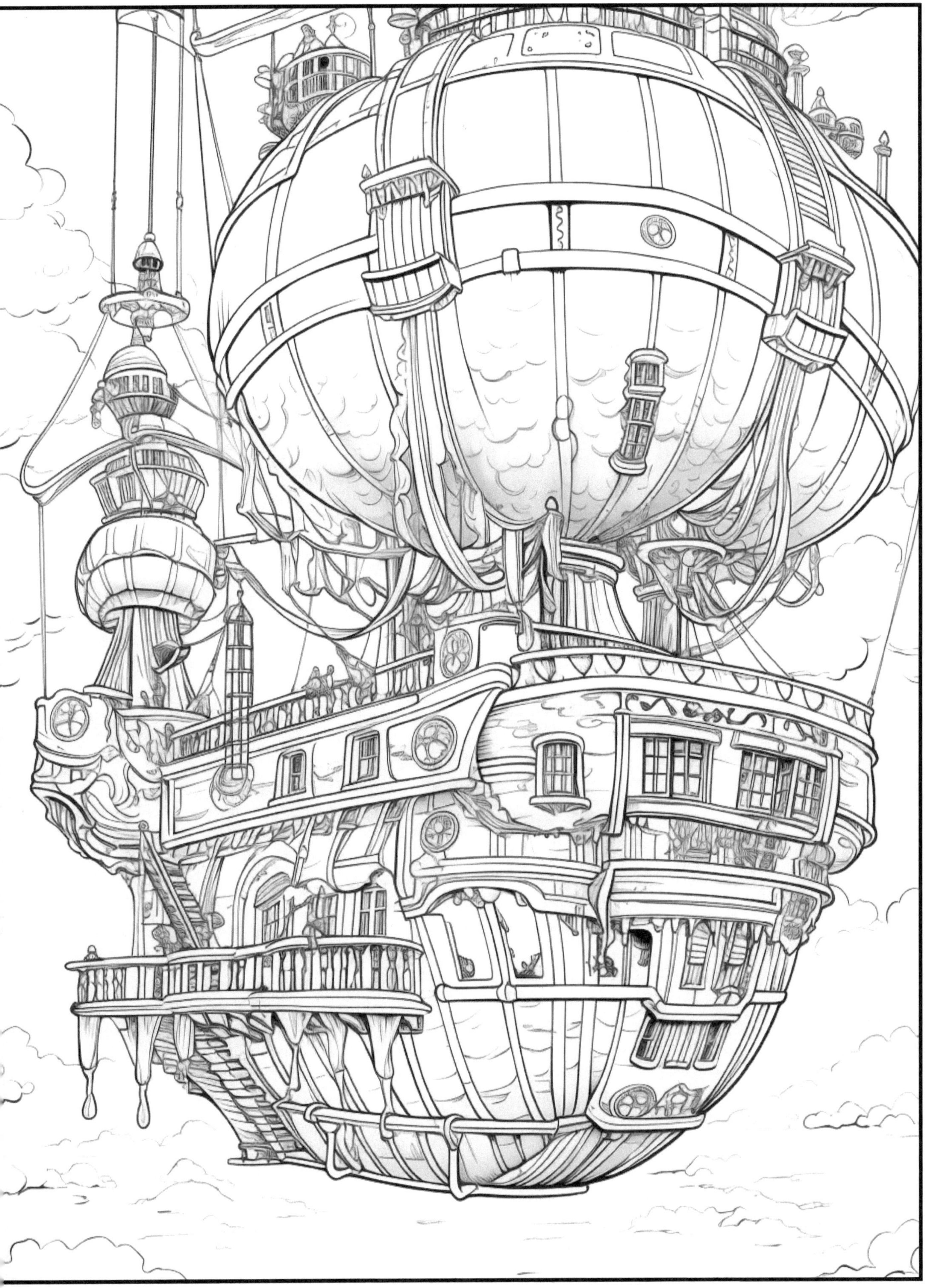

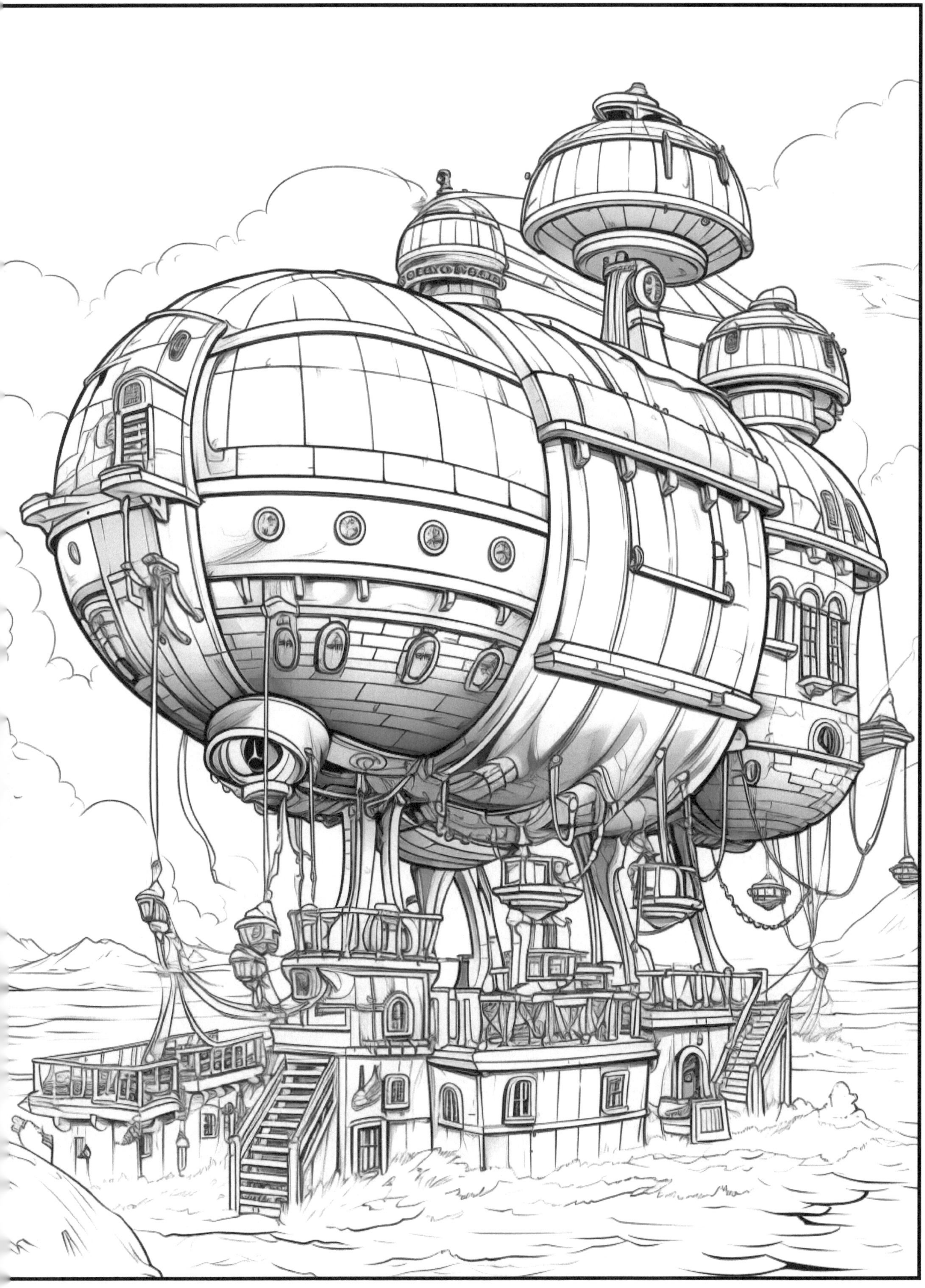

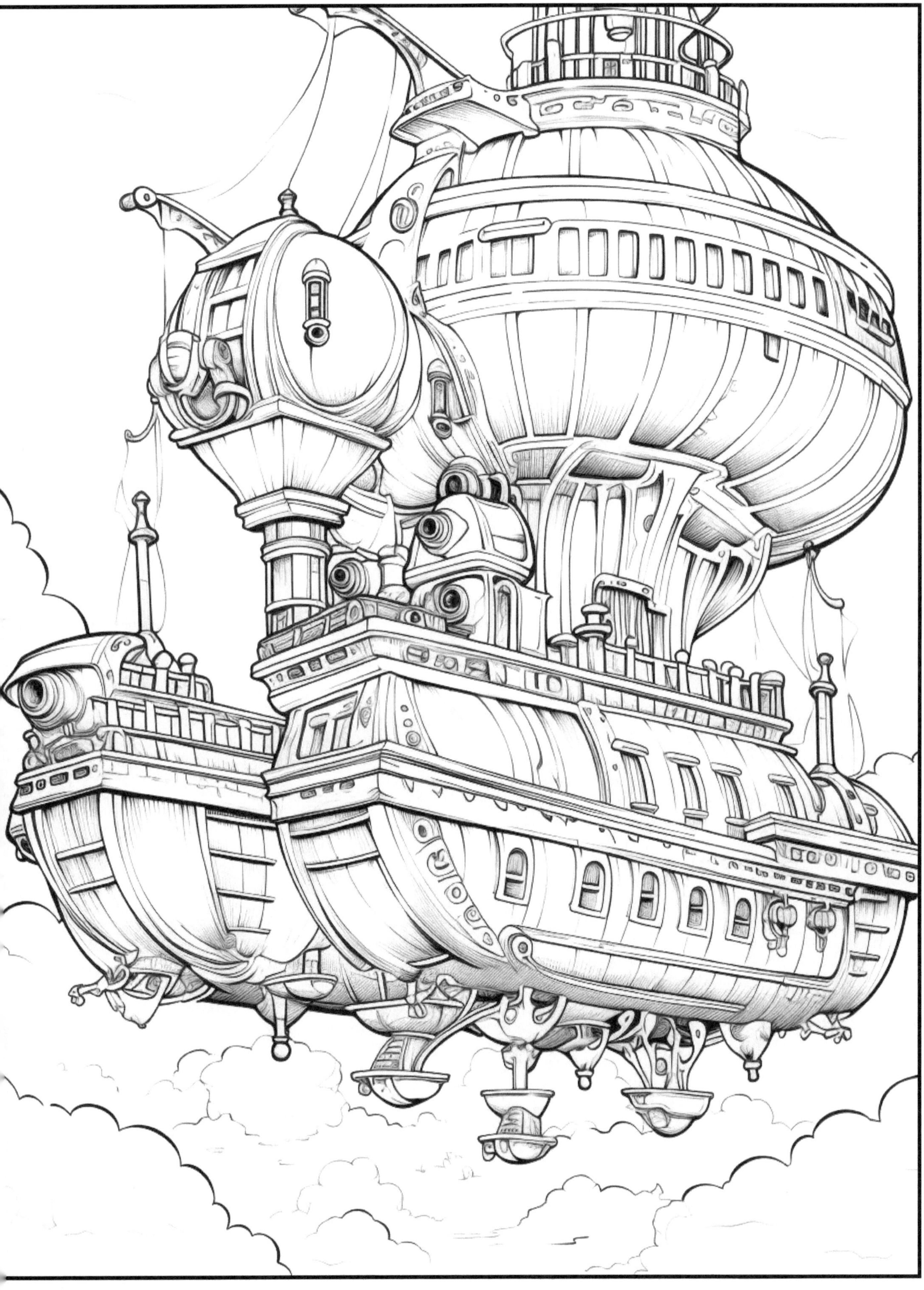

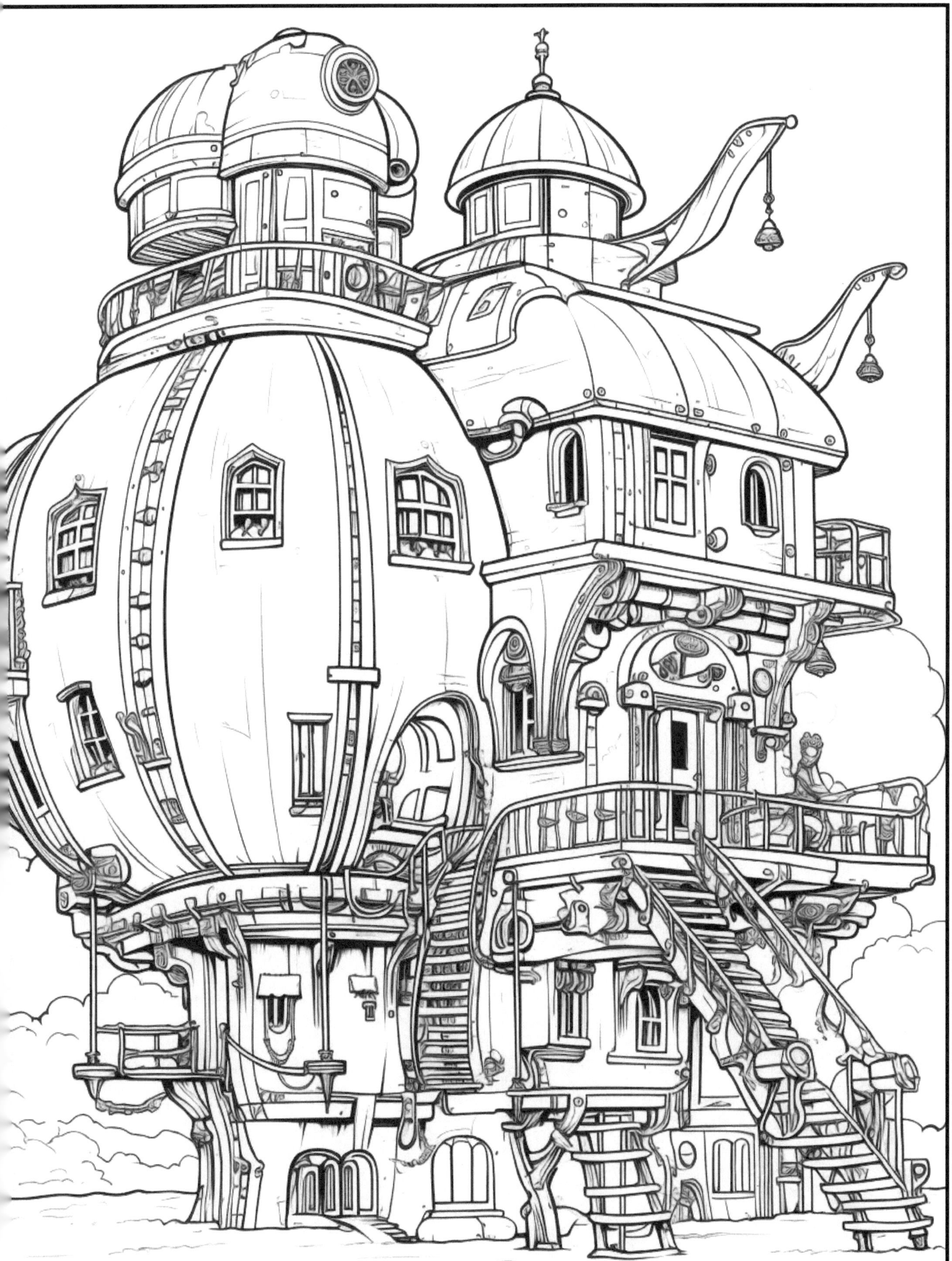

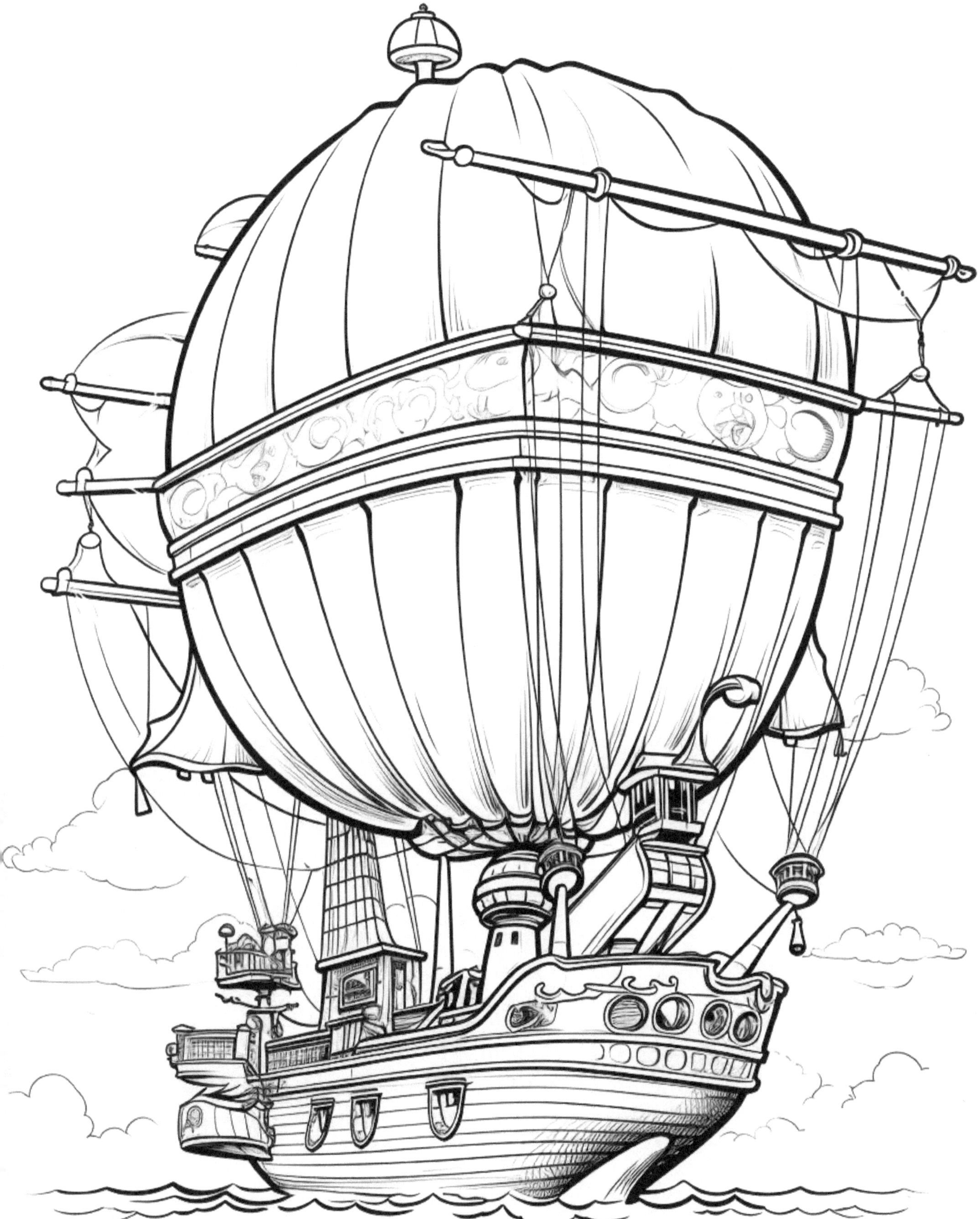

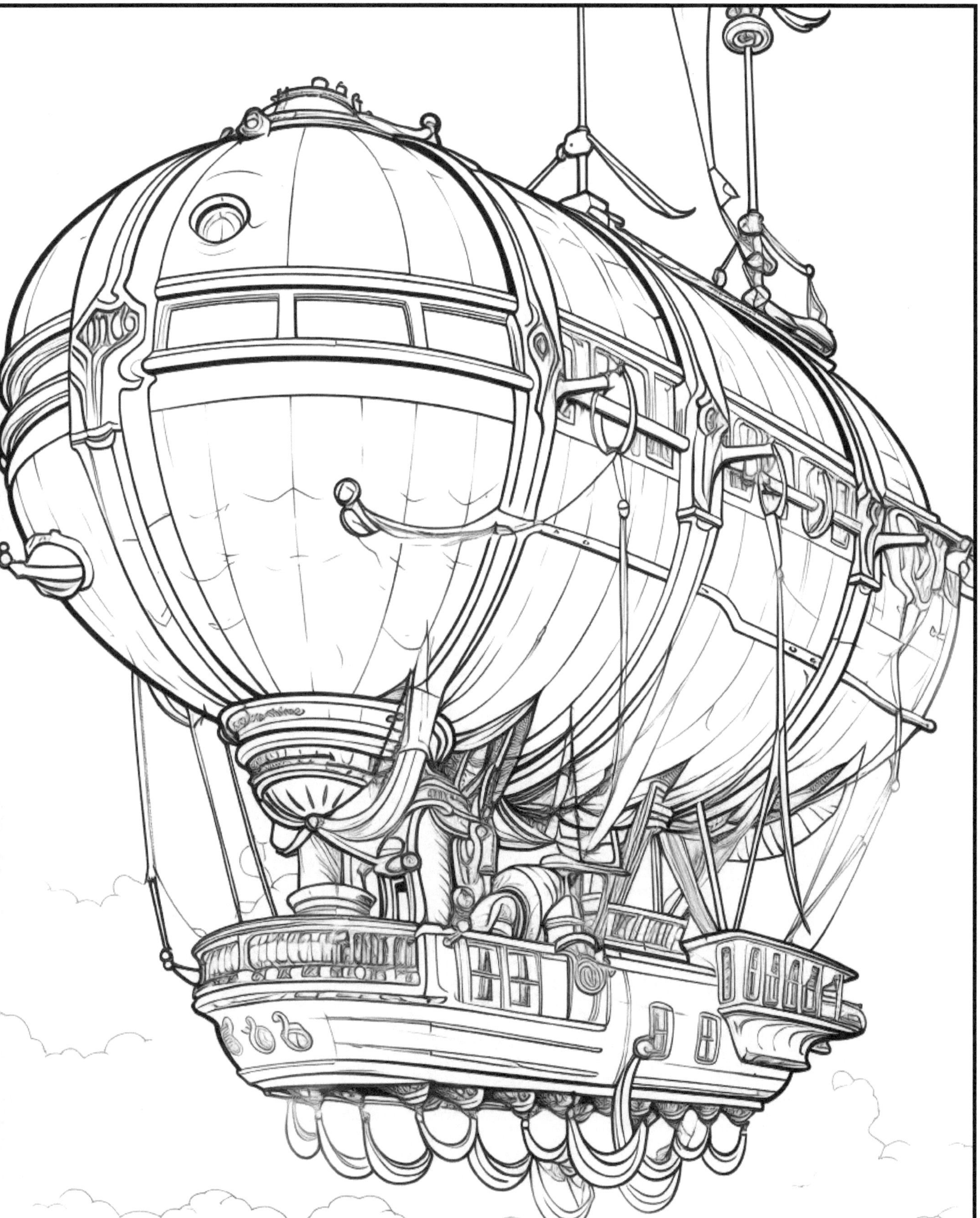

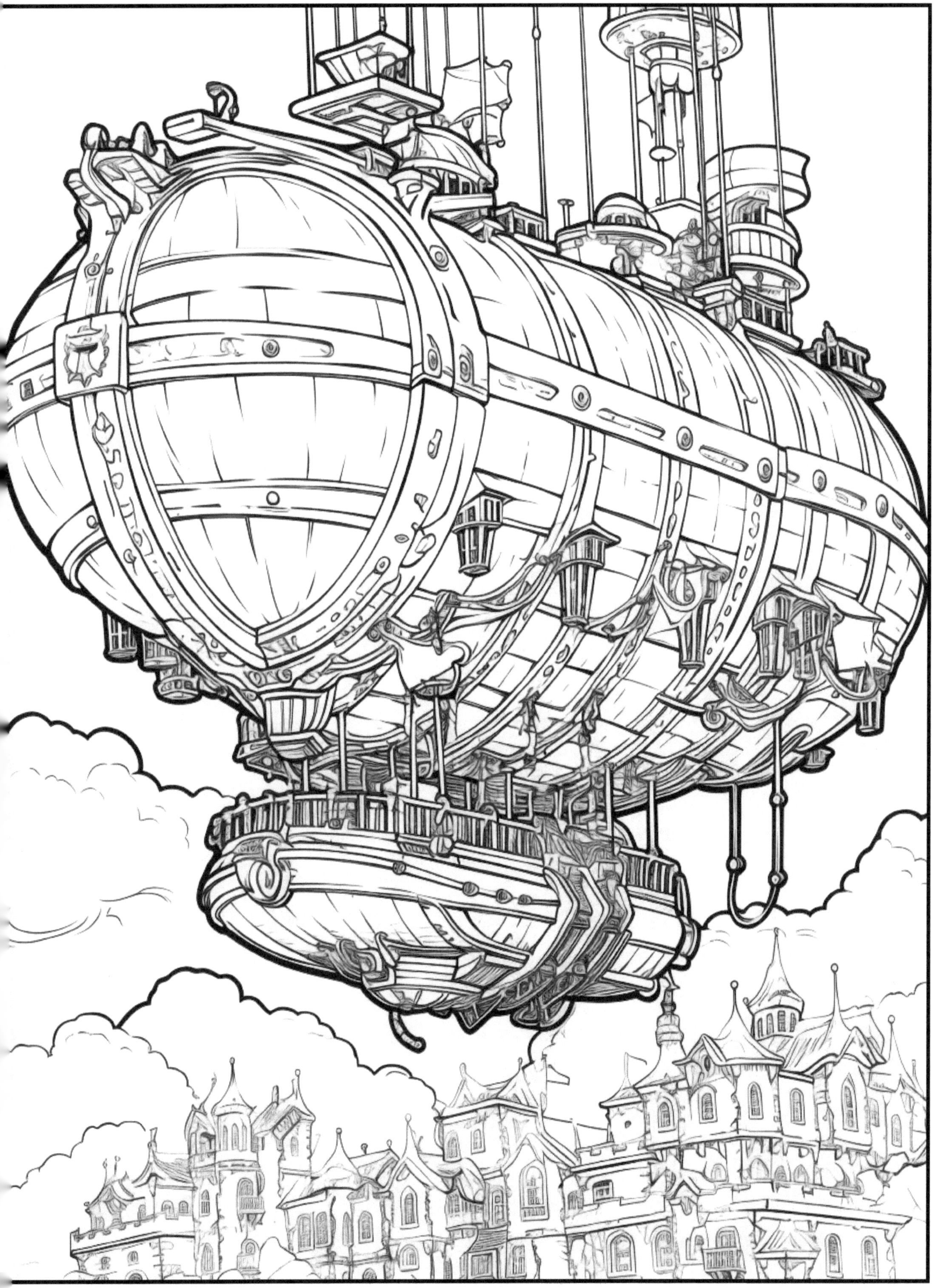

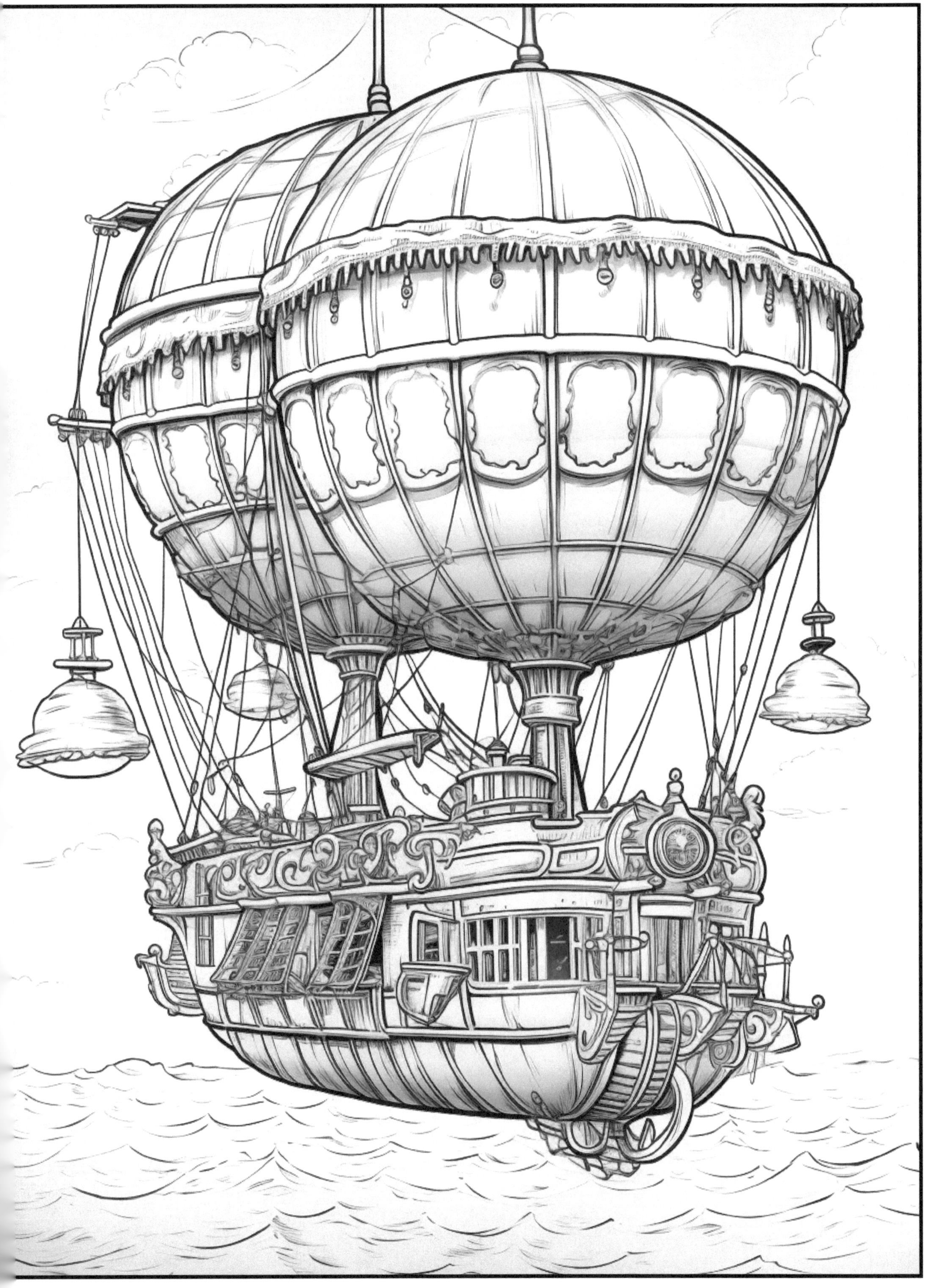

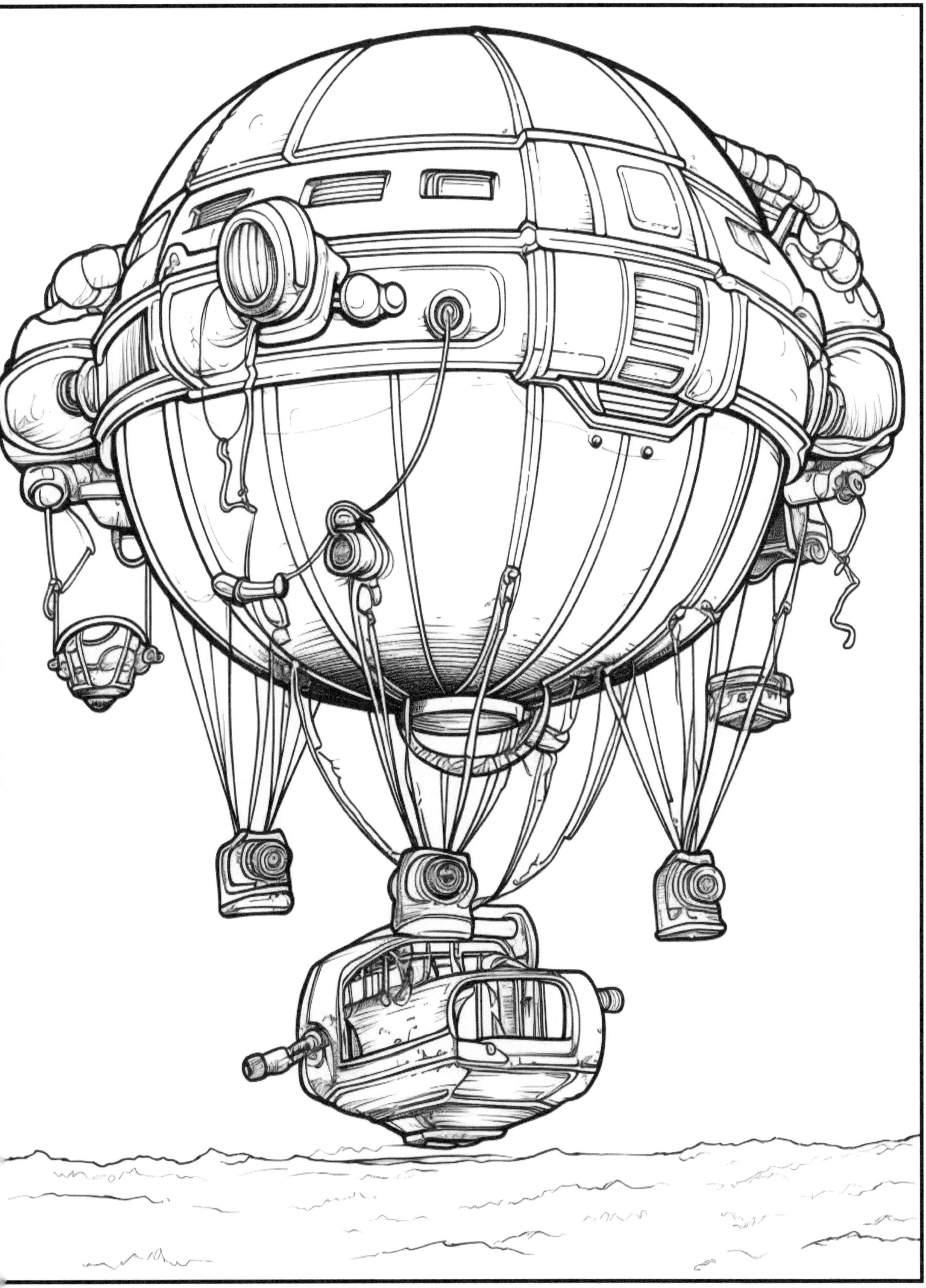

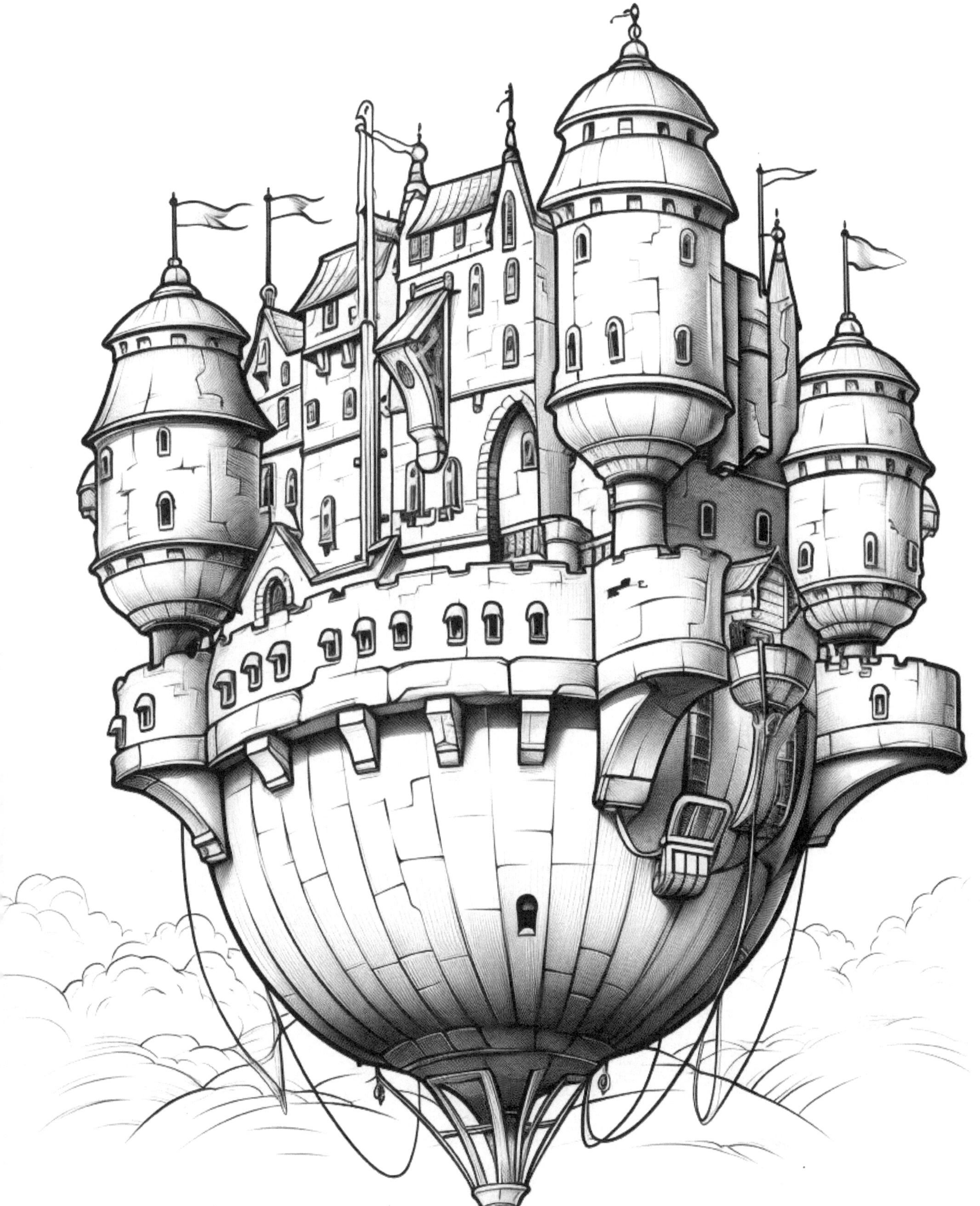

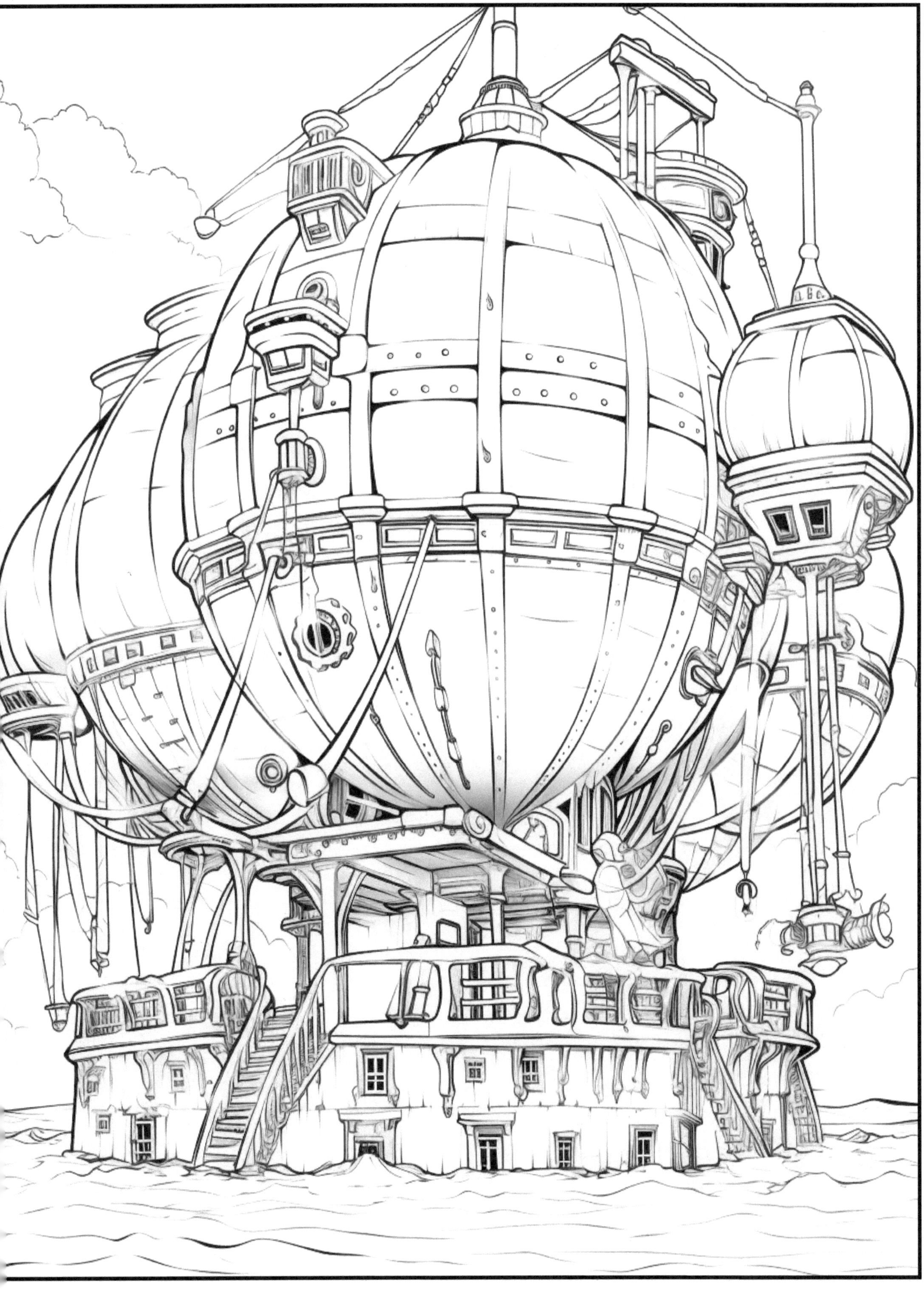

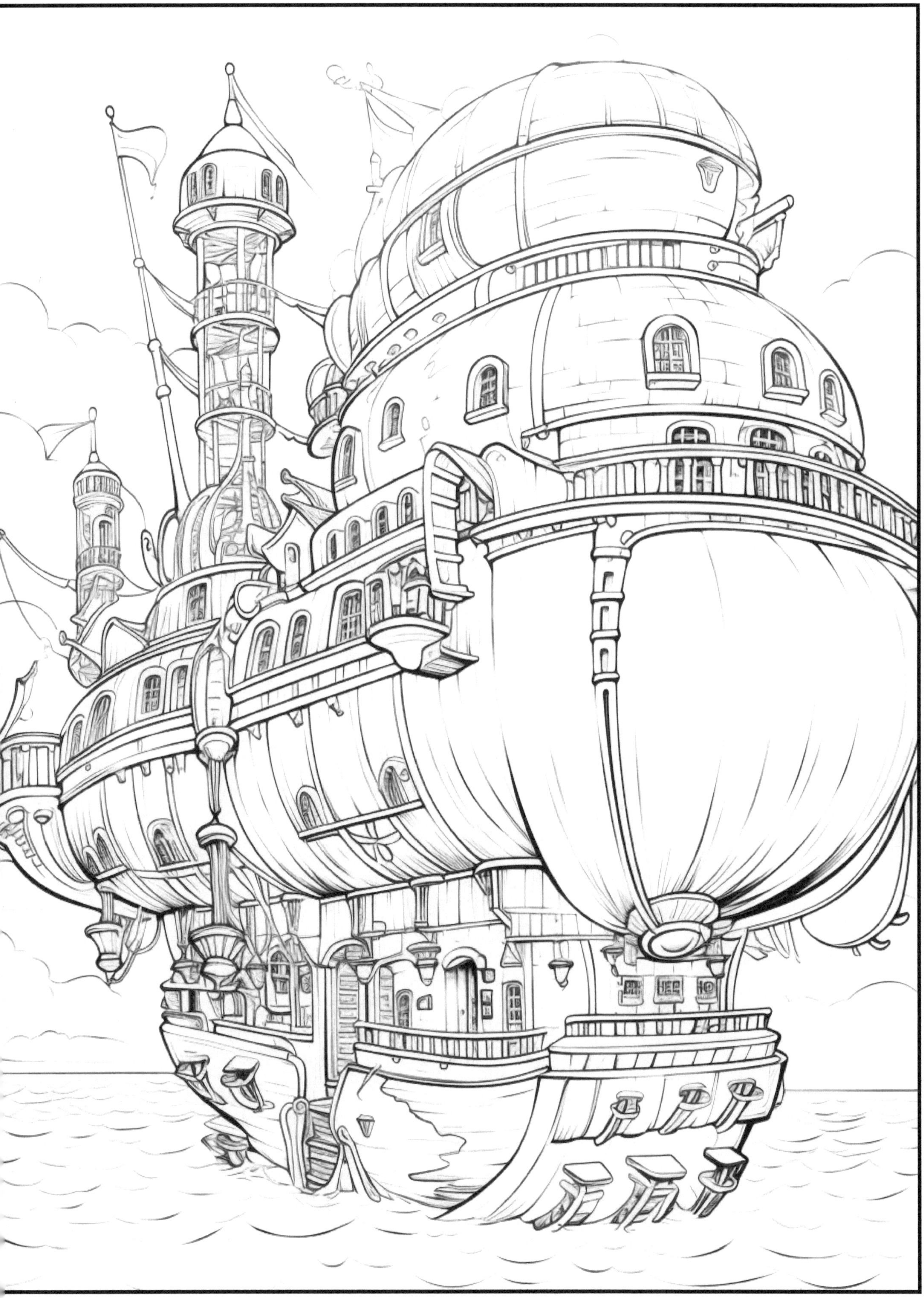

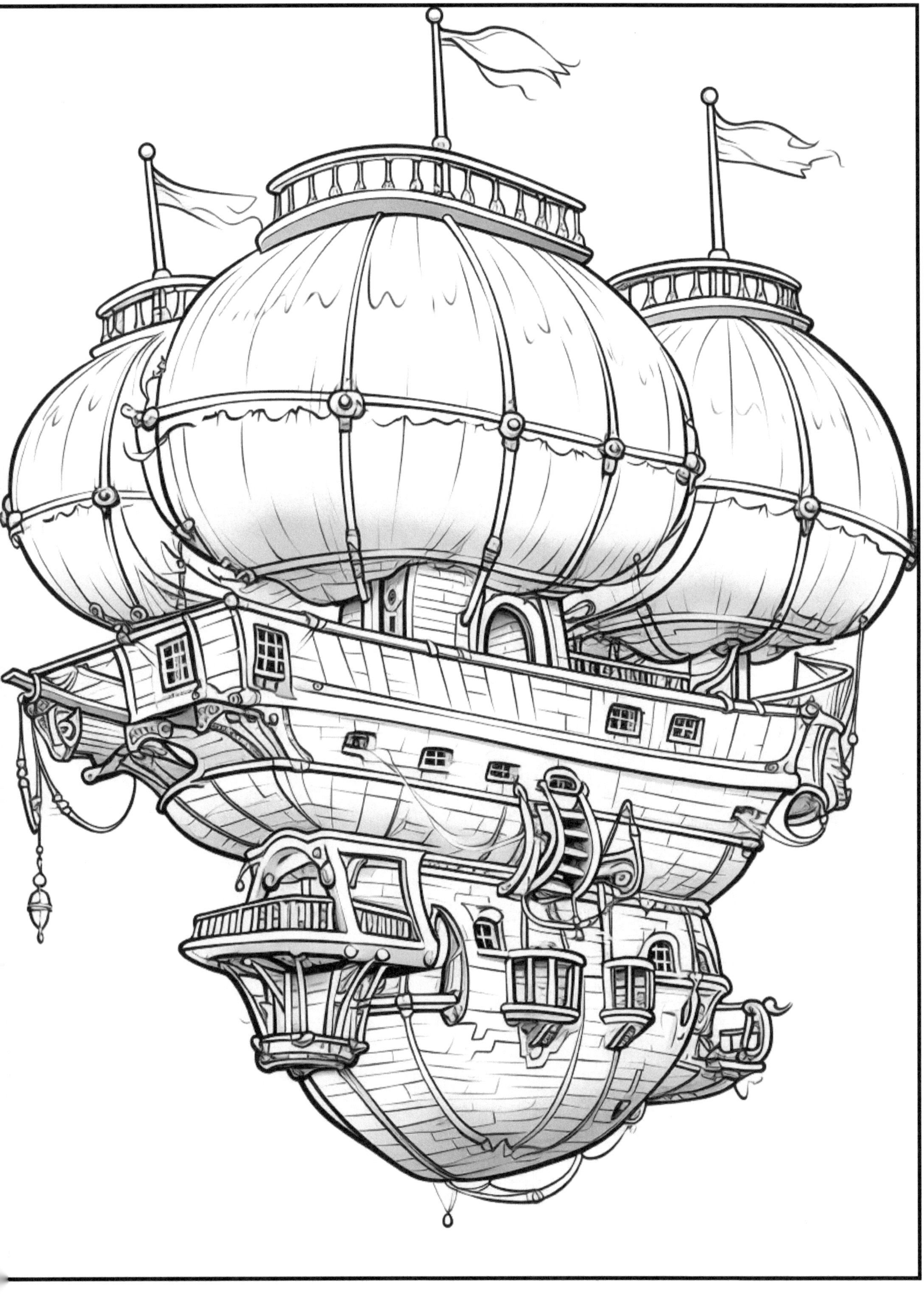

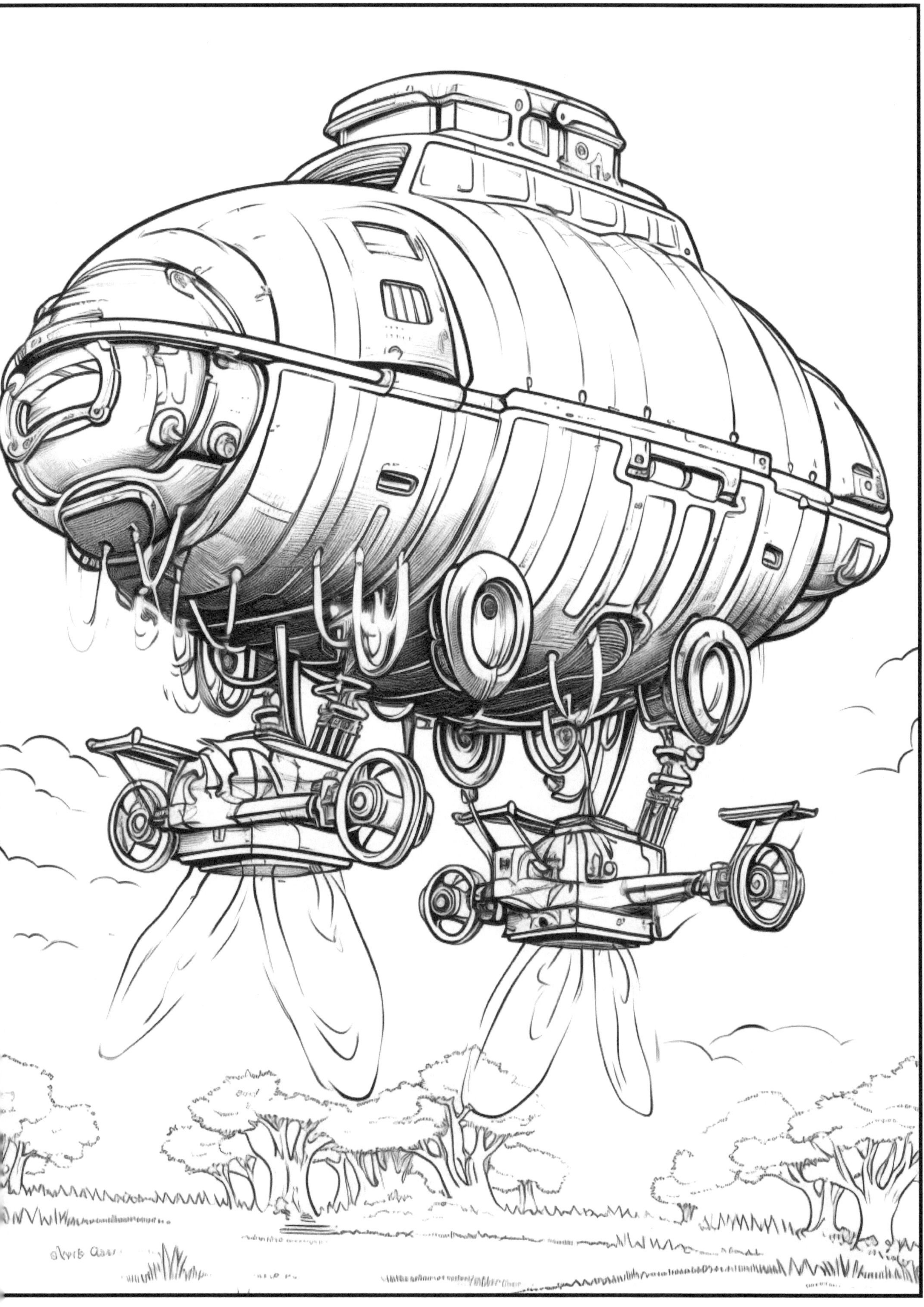

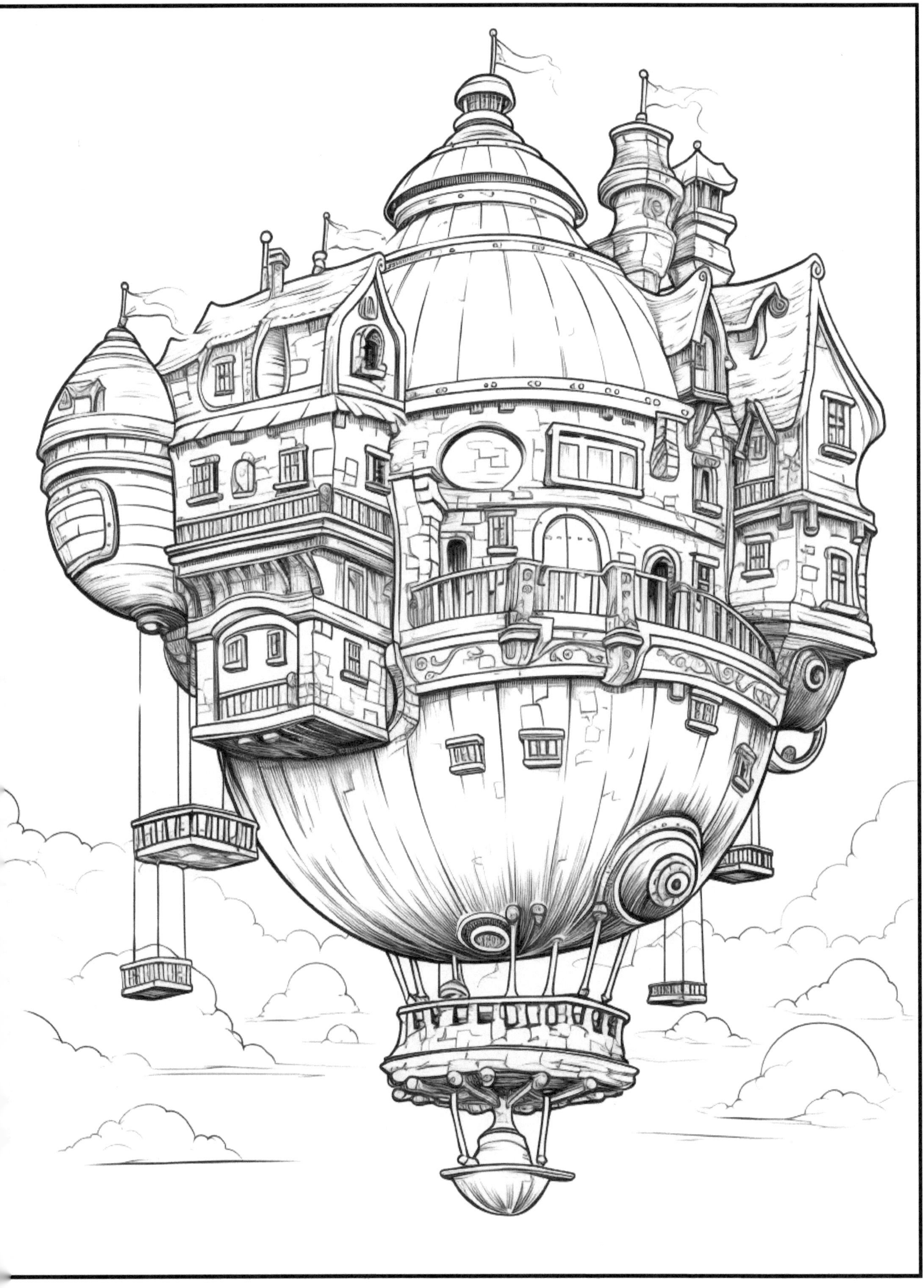

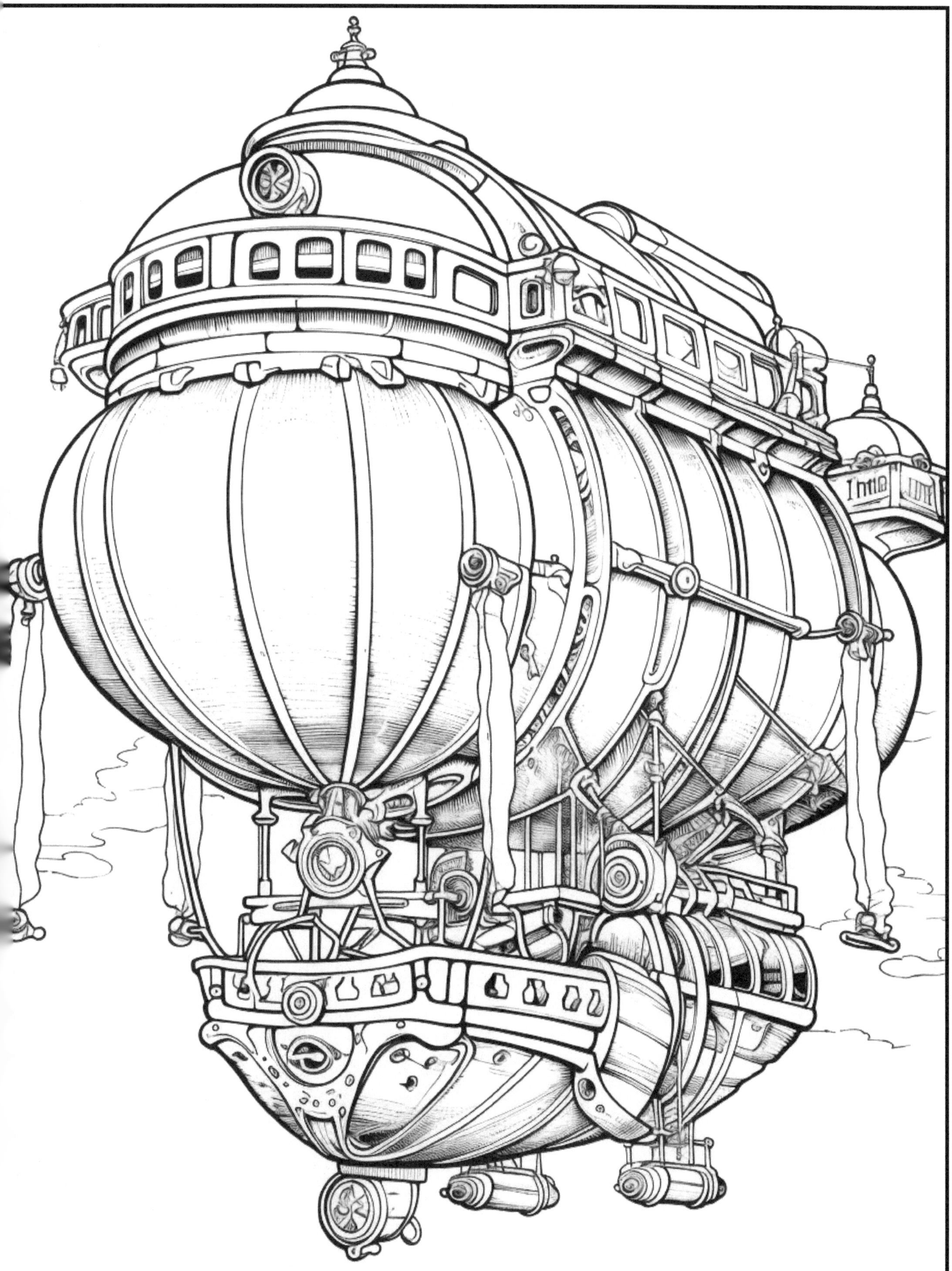

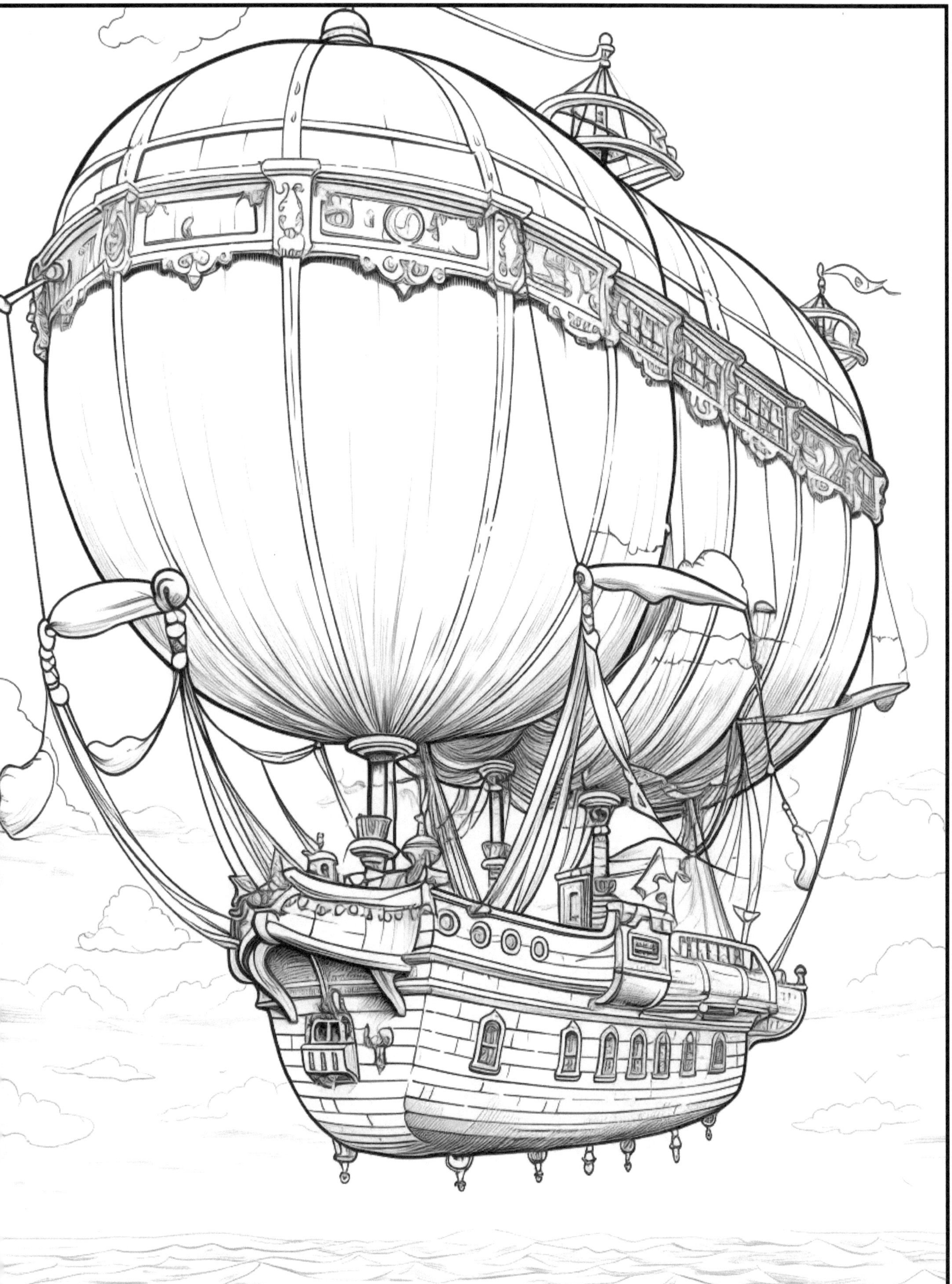

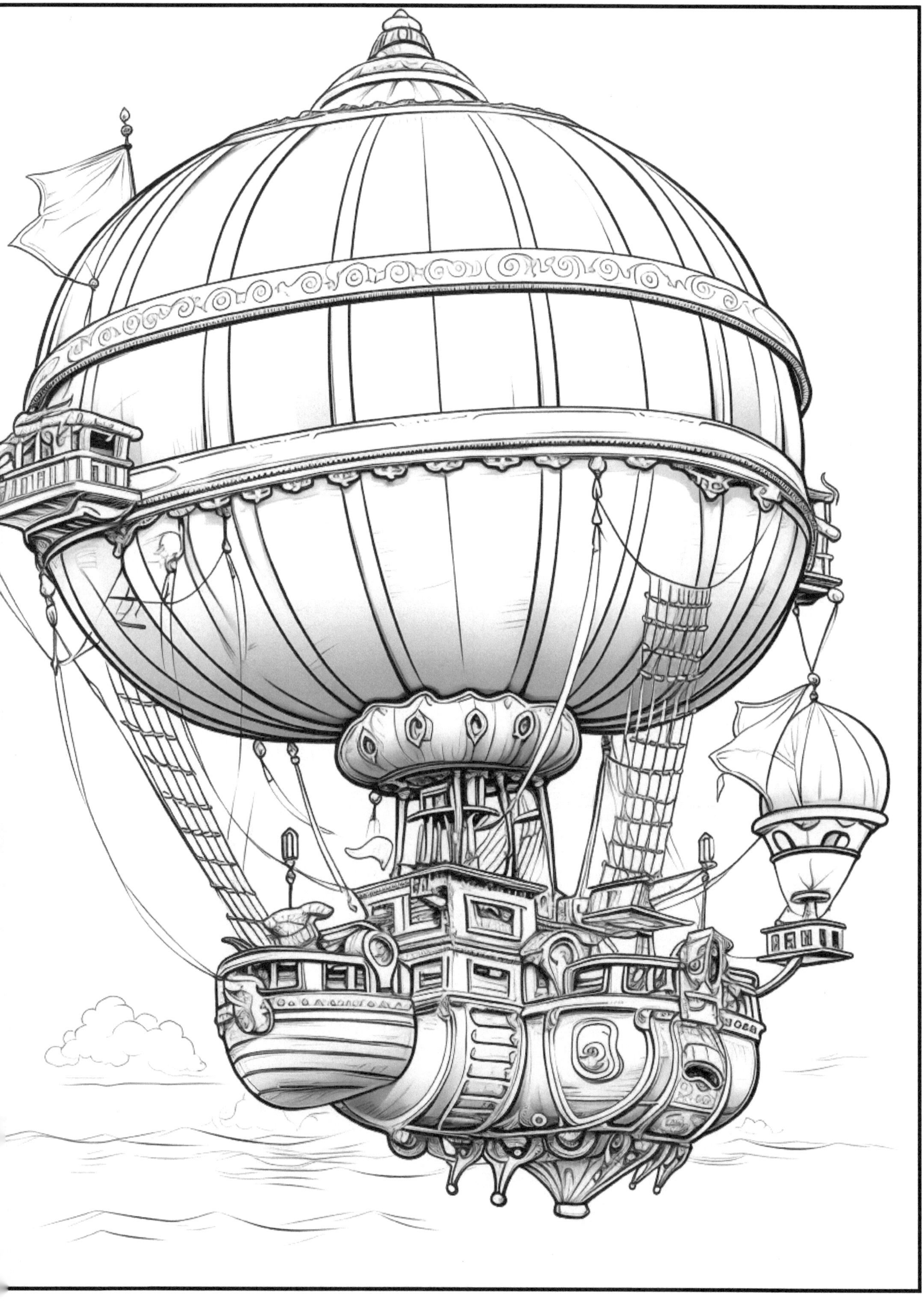

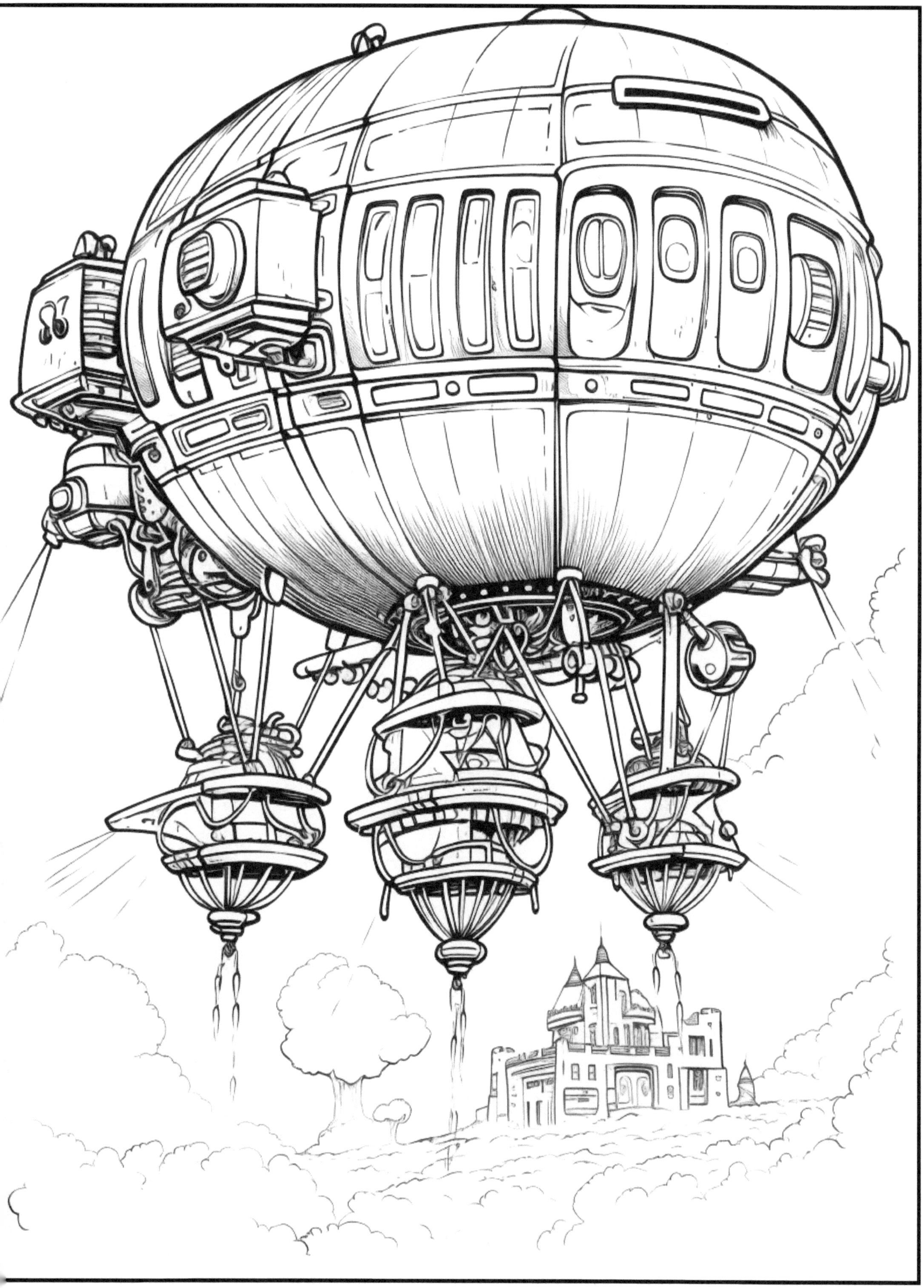

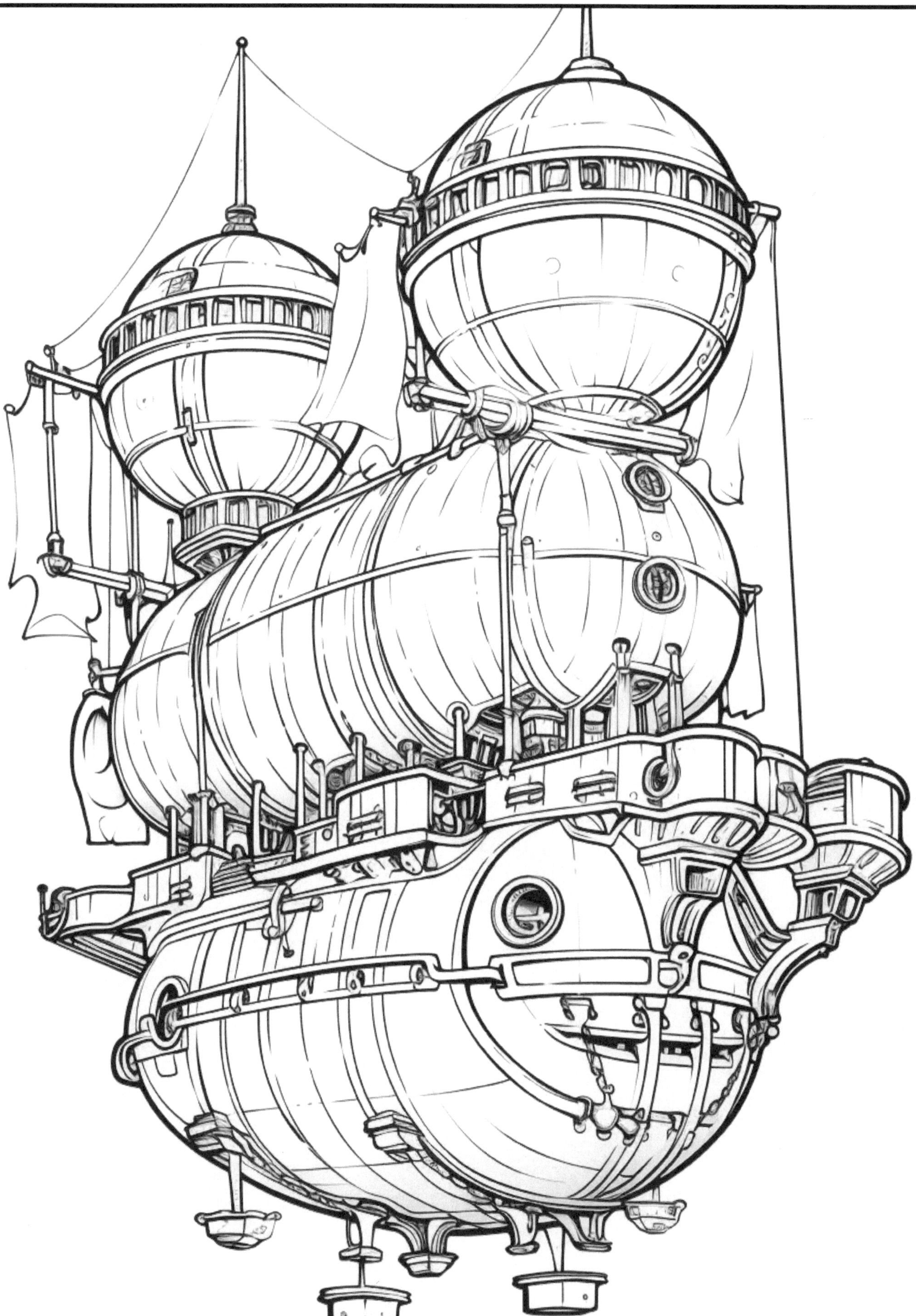

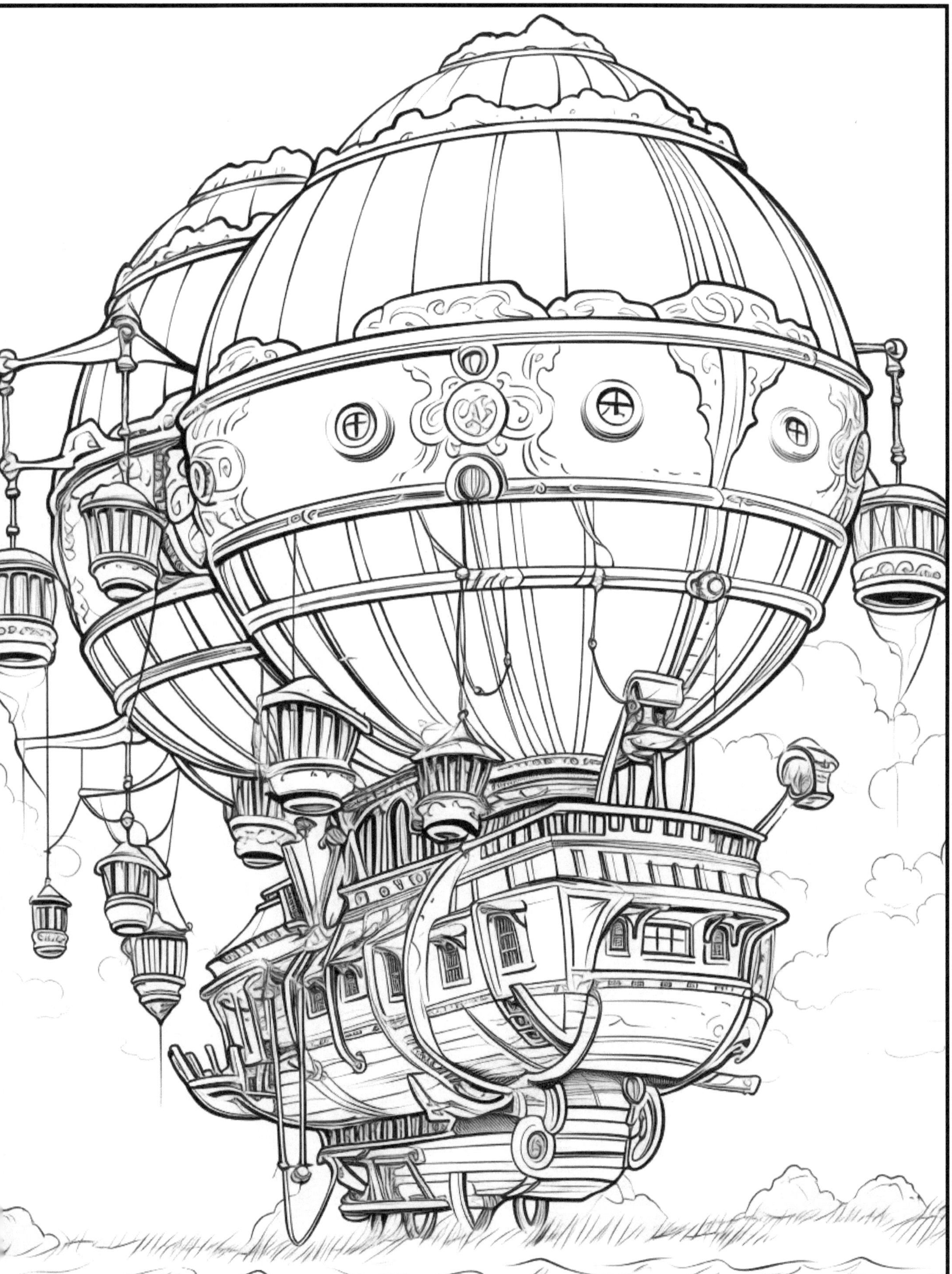

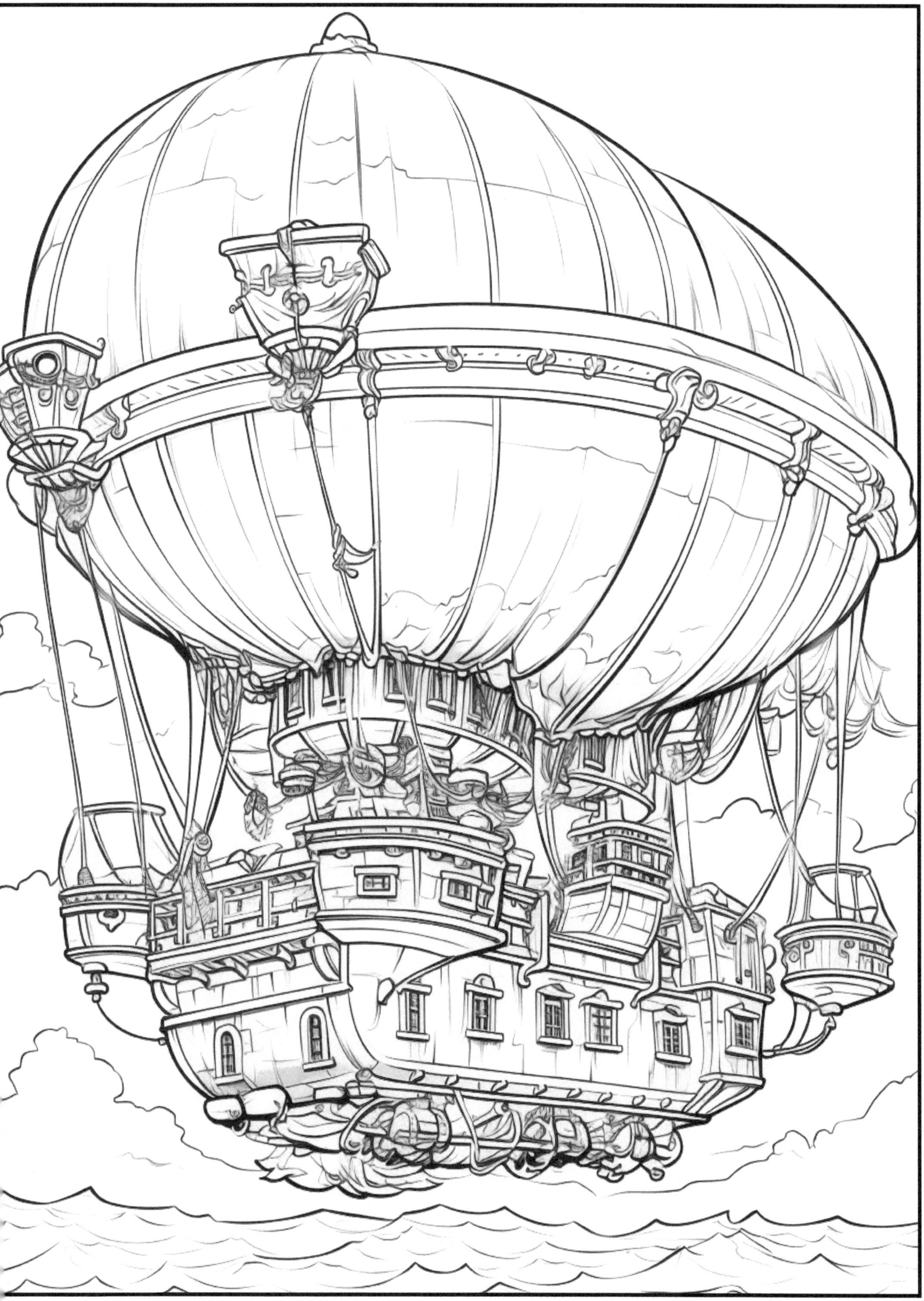

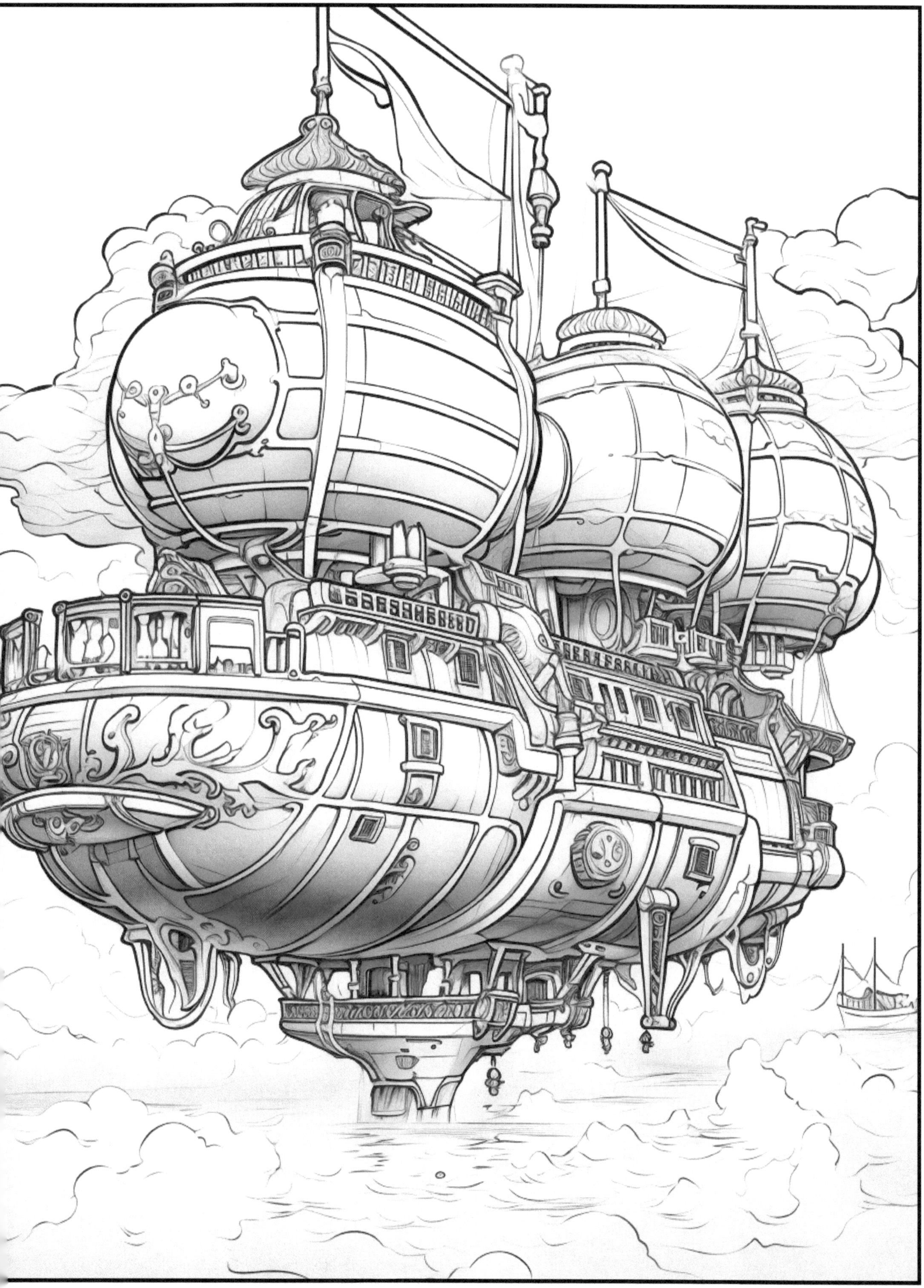

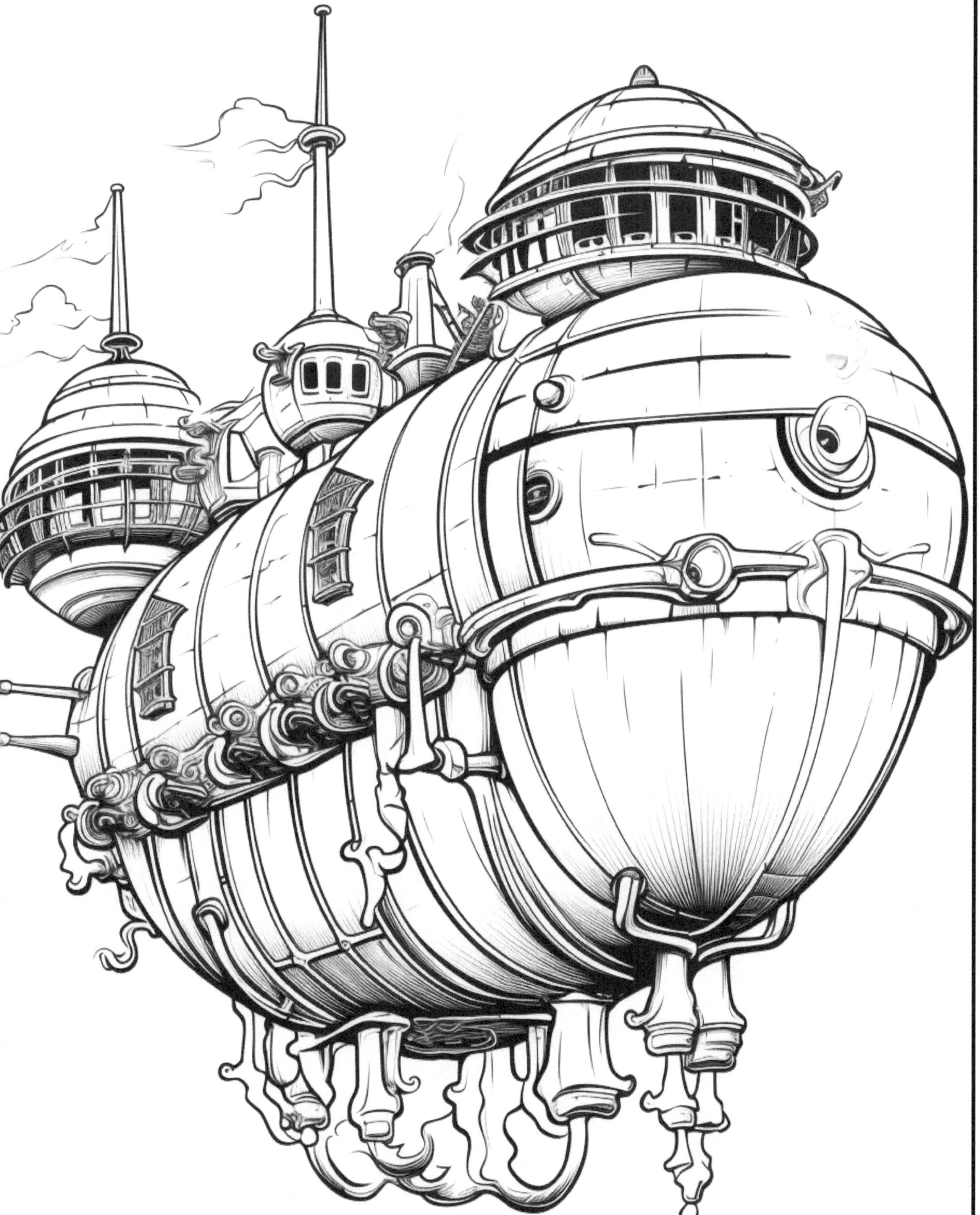

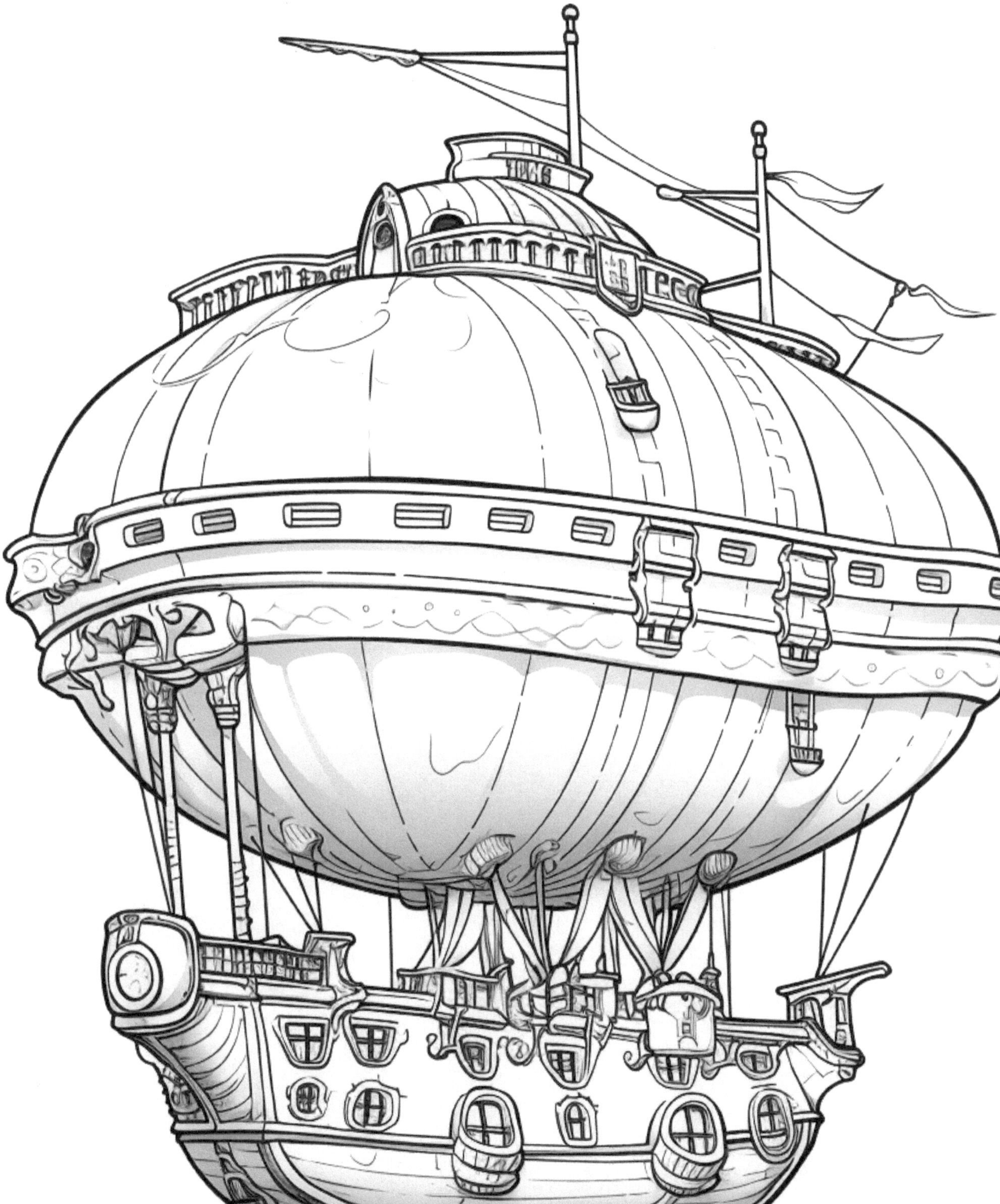

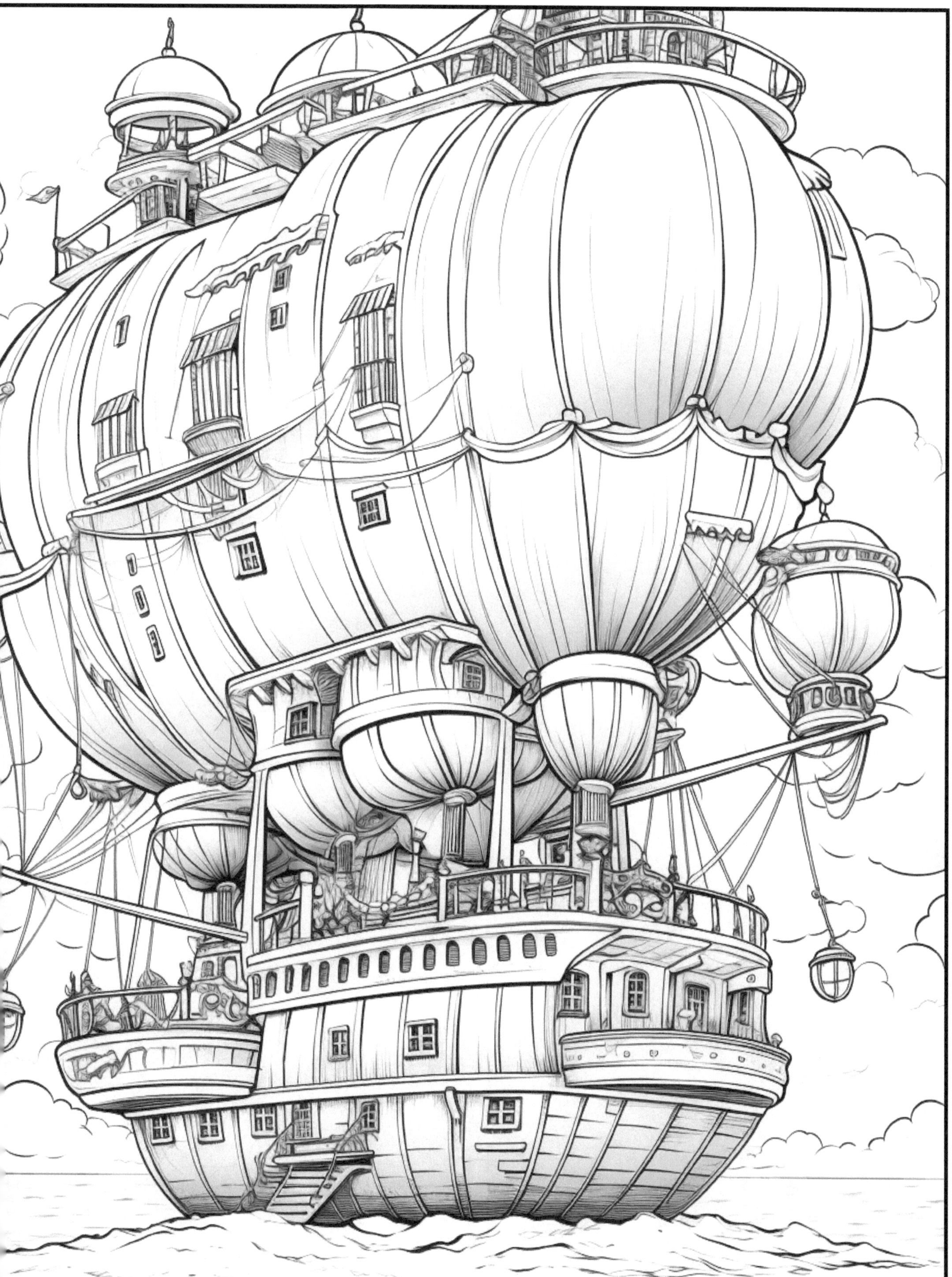

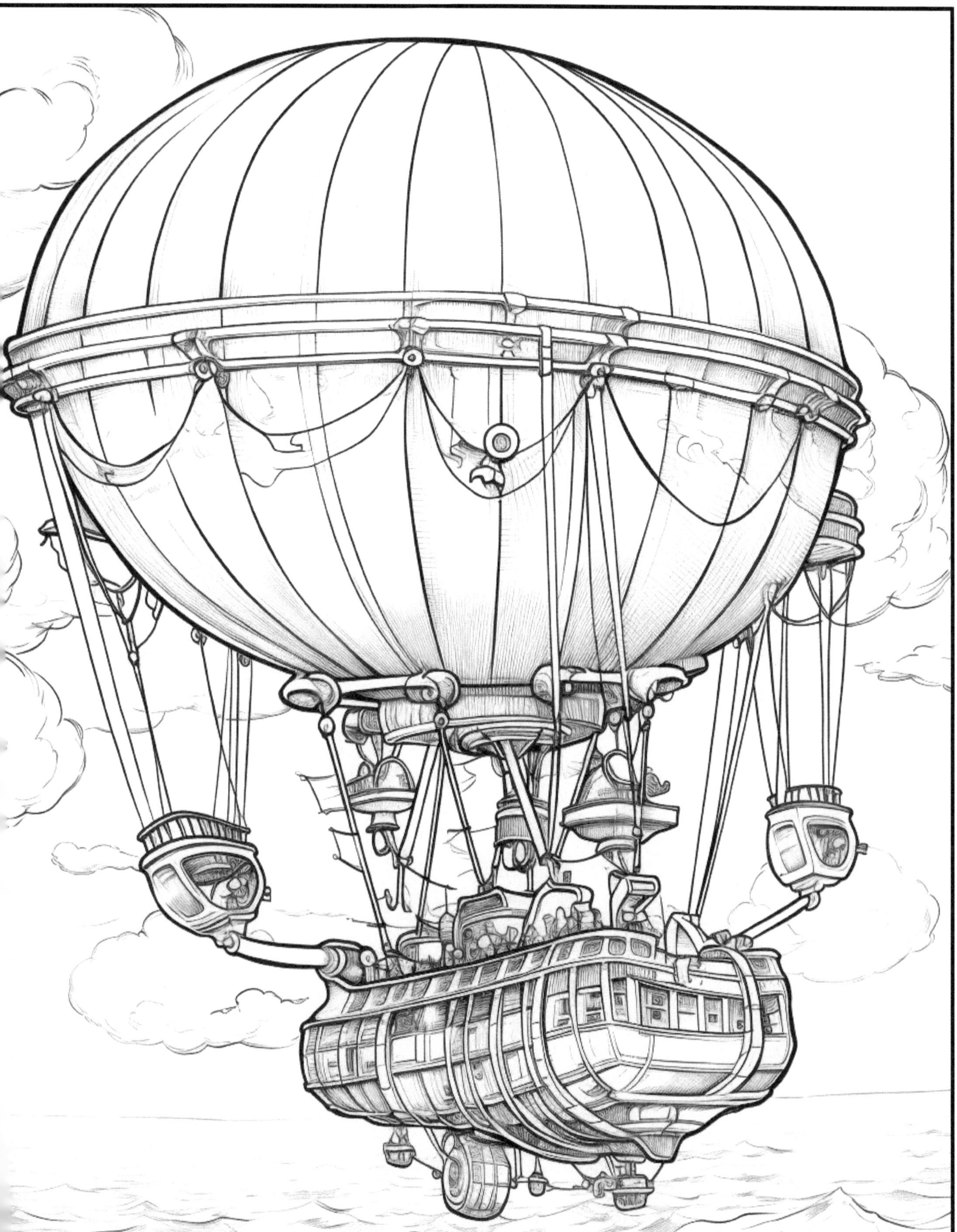

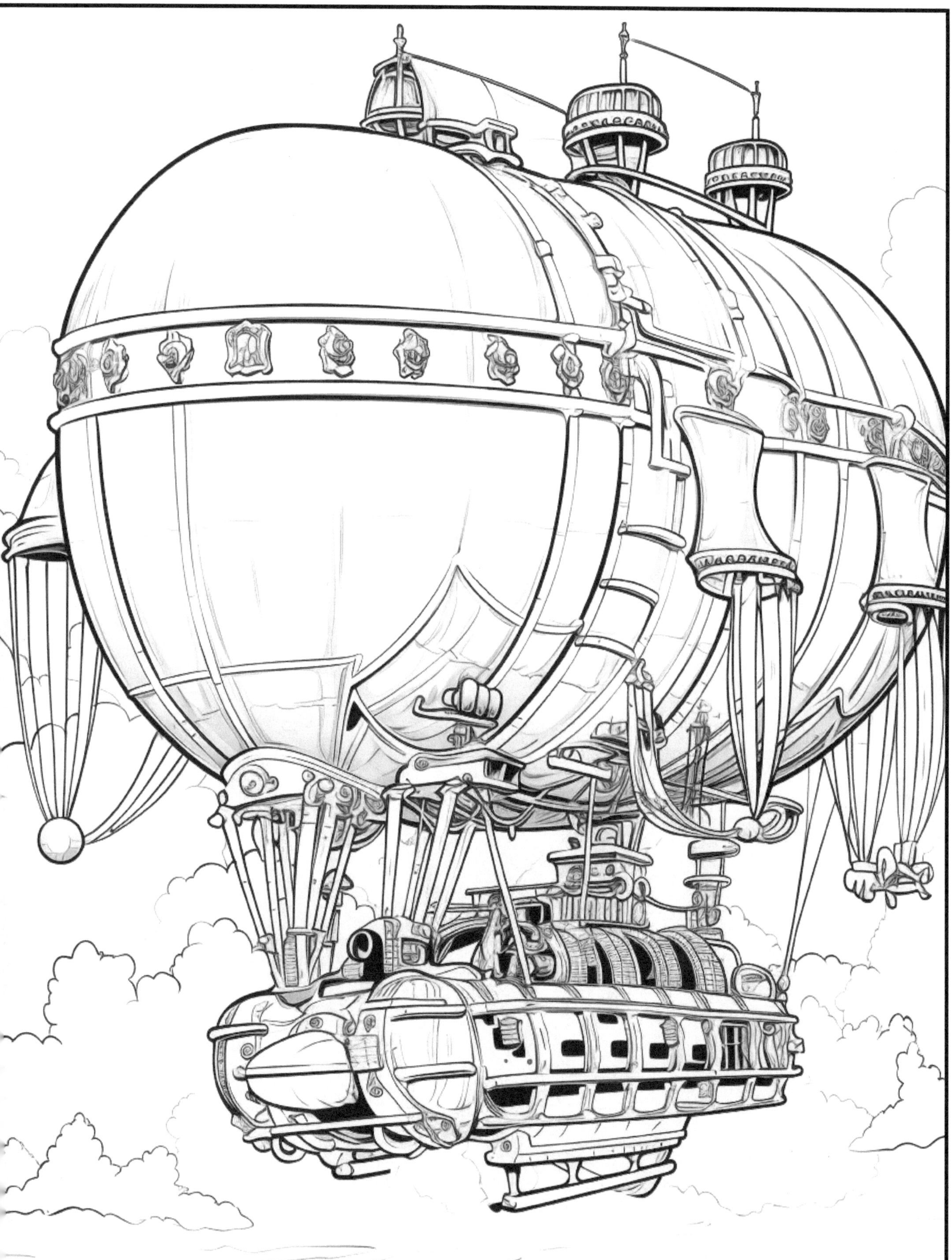

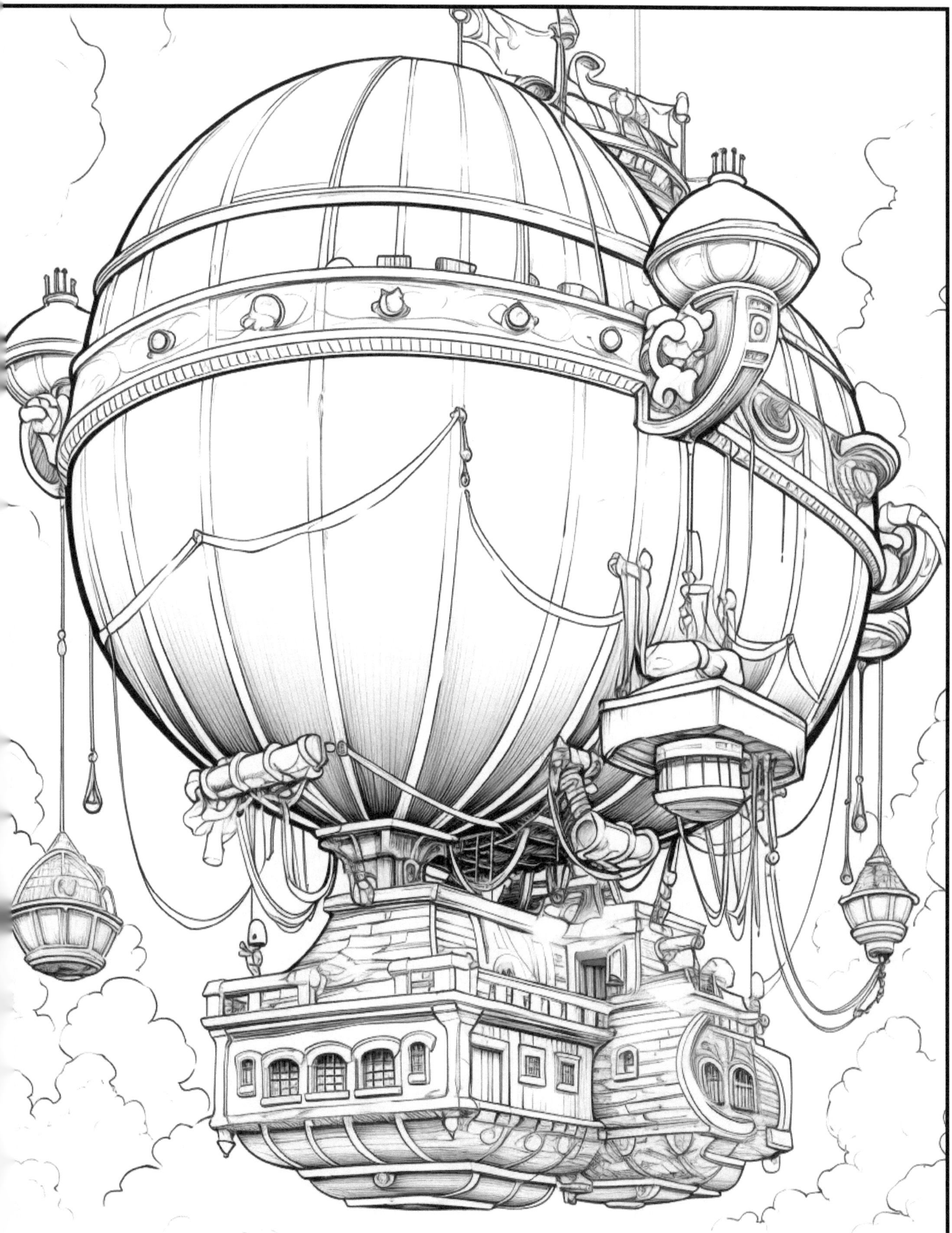

Made in United States
Troutdale, OR
05/30/2024

20215039R00058